**Guide to Domestic
Building Surveys**

Butterworth Architecture Management Guides

1 The Architect's Guide to Running a
Job
Ronald Green
2 Standard Letters in Architectural
Practice
David Chappell
3 Standard Letters for Building
Contractors
David Chappell
4 The Architect in Employment
David Chappell

Butterworth Architecture Legal Guides

1 Professional Liability 2nd edition
Ray Cecil
2 Building Contract Dictionary
Vincent Powell-Smith and
David Chappell
3 JCT Intermediate Form of Contract
David Chappell and
Vincent Powell-Smith
4 Small Works Contract
Documentation
Jack Bowyer
5 JCT Minor Works Form of Contract
David Chappell and
Vincent Powell-Smith

Construction Law Reports

Volumes 1 – 12 edited by Michael
Furmston and Vincent Powell-Smith

Guide to Domestic Building Surveys

Fourth edition

Jack Bowyer Dipl Arch (Leeds)

Butterworth Architecture
London Boston Singapore Sydney Toronto Wellington

Butterworth Architecture
is an imprint of Butterworth Scientific

First edition published by The Architectural Press,
1971
Second edition, 1972
Third edition, 1979
Fourth edition, 1988

© **Jack Bowyer, 1988**

British Library Cataloguing in Publication Data
Bowyer, Jack
    Guide to domestic building surveys. — 4th edn.
    1. Dwellings—Testing 2. Building inspection
    I. Title
    692   TH 4817.5

ISBN 0 408 50000 X

Typeset by S & P Business Systems,
Graphic House, Chipstead, Surrey.
Printed and bound by Hartnolls Ltd.,
Bodmin, Cornwall.

Contents

Introduction

The value of a property is dependent on many factors. One of these is its structural condition. Prospective purchasers require such surveys to be carried out for a number of reasons:

○ To establish that the property is structurally sound
○ That it is likely to survive without undue structural maintenance for a reasonable number of years relative to its age on purchase.
○ To satisfy the finance organisation funding the purchase that the property is structurally sound.

This book deals with the kind of survey a private house buyer would expect to be carried out to provide him with a report enabling him to decide whether the property is in such a condition as to be worth buying. This must not be confused with surveys carried out by Building Societies, which, in the main, are to enable them to ensure that the property is in such a condition and situation as to be a reasonable security for loan purposes.

The private structural survey must incorporate certain specific matters that are of prime importance to the prospective purchaser:

○ Detailed advice on the structural condition of the property. Advice on the condition and likely efficiency of the drainage and services.
○ Advice on the thermal efficiency of the structure and its components.
○ An estimate of the probable cost of remedying any defects reported, and
○ Advice on the future maintenance costs of the property.

It is unlikely that any purchaser will set out his requirements in such a fashion, but it is probable that he will ask for specific matters to be investigated. Great care must be taken in carrying out the inspection and preparing the report to ensure that all such items are fully investigated and attention drawn in the report to the findings and conclusions reached.

Valuations are often requested with the report. Property valuation is a very specialised branch of practice and unless the surveyor feels adequate to such work, especially in areas of the country where he does not normally practise, he should advise his client to employ a local valuer for such a service. The extent of the surveyor's services should be made quite clear to his client. 'Quickie' or brief reports are always unsatisfactory and such work should be rejected: it can only lead to omissions or wrong conclusions and possible future litigation.

Fees should be agreed at the time the commission is accepted. Assessment of costs is often difficult unless the building is well known or situated close to base. The use of hourly rate charges is probably the fairest method of fee assessment, based on rates recommended by the appropriate professional institution. Any difficulty experienced in the recovery of fees from clients would, in such circumstances, be sympathetically considered by the courts.

The law and the survey

No professional body defines the exact responsibilities of the surveyor carrying out a structural survey. Building Societies rely on corporate membership of one of the professions directly concerned with the building industry as a test of professional competence. Case law is scarce. A number of factors must be considered:

○ The intending purchaser is entitled to expect that the survey will expose any defects likely to materially affect the life and value of the building.

○ Failure to find and comment on such defects would be held to show a lack of professional competence.

○ Clear instructions should be included in the brief to check for and report on minor defects which could not materially affect the life of the building.

○ The extent and scope of the survey should be agreed in writing.

Most building structures include a number of voids, either as part of a structural element or casing to a service. These may conceal defects or structural deterioration which may not be apparent and only come to light subsequent to the survey. These include:

○ Woodworm infestation in timber floors.

○ Dry rot in voids under suspended ground floors.

○ Defective jointing between one-pipe stacks and soil drain bends under suspended ground floors.

○ Leaks in ducted service pipe work.

At any suggestion of such a defect the surveyor's responsibility is to advise his client of the need to open up the structure to investigate the possibility of defect. The courts have

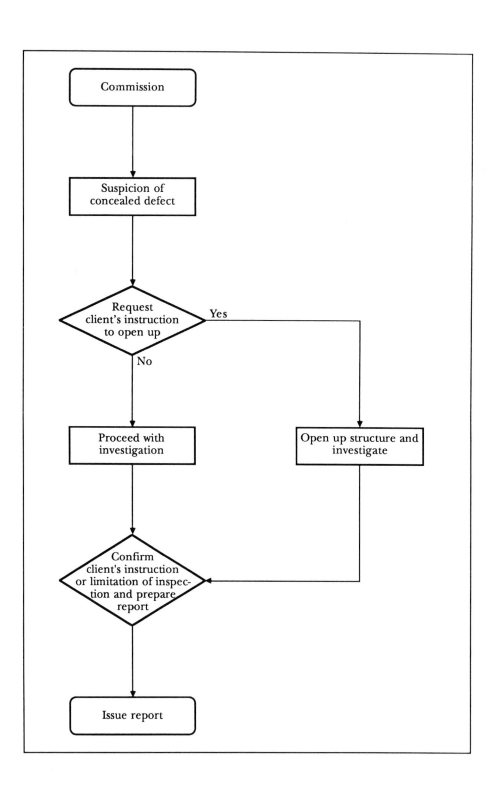

held that:

○ It is not the duty of the surveyor to lift floor coverings or make detailed examination of enclosed portions of the building.

○ The onus is however on the surveyor to make sure he investigates any suspicious circumstances.

○ His care in so doing is evidence of his competence in carrying out the work.

To avoid costly disputes in connection with latent defects the surveyor must clearly state in his report:

○ The limitation of his inspection, or

○ The confirmation of the client's instruction or decision.

○ The weather at the time of the inspection.

The discovery of any serious defect unknown to the vendor should be pointed out to him without expressing any opinion on the matter.

Equipment

Equipment needed to carry out the inspection falls into three categories:
○ That provided by the builder to carry out his duties in providing attendance and in connection with the drain test.
○ That provided by the specialists to enable them to carry out the required tests on the electrical installation, etc.
○ That needed by the surveyor as personal equipment to enable him to carry out his specific tasks and to record the results of his findings.

So far as equipment is necessary to carry out builder's attendance and specialist testing, this will be provided by those concerned and the surveyor will be employing only those who are fully conversant with their specific requirements. Where any special items will be needed and anticipated by the surveyor, these should be brought to their attention when the order for the work is placed. For example, extra-long ladders might be needed to reach certain parts of the building. Most surveyors have found from experience that certain items of equipment are essential to their work and while there are particular preferences for particular makes of equipment, most are agreed on a basic list. Most items are readily available from hardware shops with the exception of the moisture meter which is usually obtained from a specialist supplier.

The following is a list of equipment which, by experience, has been found to cover most eventualities. The list includes some practical applications and hints to enable the surveyor to use the tools with maximum efficiency and with the minimum of damage to the structure and finishings:

○ A stout clipboard to hold the check list during the survey. Pens are continually being misplaced and a Parker Slinger is recommended for note taking.

○ A stout electric torch, preferably of the rubber cased pattern. This is preferable because hard usage and the likelihood of being dropped from heights does not appear to reduce its useful and effective life.

○ A stout bradawl is useful for testing timbers for rot, floor boards for defects, mortar joints for sulphate attack and has many other uses. When using a bradawl it is unacceptable to lay waste the suspect joinery and timbers in the search for defects. As in all matters of this sort there are right and wrong ways to proceed and the following is suggested:

> When using a bradawl to check for timber defects insert the point either into the underside, the edge or a joint between members. The small hole will then be almost invisible. Always insert the point into shrinkage cracks or the throating of a sill when testing for rot.

○ A stout screwdriver for levering up boarded access traps to check timbers for infestation, etc. This tool is also useful for clearing mud from manhole cover frame joints and lifting edges. When levering access traps insert the blade into the header joint which will reduce the risk of the timber splitting if the trap is a tight fit.

○ A small screwdriver to remove switch plates and socket outlets to inspect the condition of the cable insulation at points most affected by room temperature. This will help to decide whether to recommend an electrical wiring test.

○ A set of manhole lifting irons. These are useful for preliminary inspections or when a cover has to be raised again after the builder has left the site. Always clear the rebates of debris before replacing the cover to ensure it returns to its proper position. Lift the cover by one end and insert a piece of timber into the gap before raising the whole – manhole covers are usually very heavy and can easily smash fingers if they slip.

○ A short spirit-level with horizontal and transverse bubbles for checking level and plumb.

○ A steel spring tape or boxwood rod for checking dimensions and the extent of defects.

○ A plumb bob and line for use with the measure to check

when the plumb of a structure needs to be specifically measured.

○ A pair of binoculars to enable roof surfaces and features, chimney stacks and other inaccessible elements to be inspected.

○ A moisture meter to check the moisture content of a material and to assist in determining whether a stain is likely to be condensation or damp penetration. When testing walls, insert the electrodes where the pinholes are unlikely to be noticed, for example at the junction of plaster and skirting.

○ A sectional or folding ladder of a size to fit inside a car boot or on the rear seat of a car. The ladder should be capable of extension to a minimum of 3 metres, preferably 4 metres, which will meet the needs of most internal domestic situations when a builder is not in attendance.

○ A camera with flashlight attachment, preferably of the 'Polaroid' type to provide visual evidence in matters which might involve dispute. A camera with reflex focusing is preferable, and a useful tip when operating in dark and confined places is to place a light-coloured object against the item to be photographed, illuminate it with a torch and focus on it.

○ A towel and soap. Structural surveys can be dirty jobs and while water can generally be obtained in empty premises, other essentials are usually lacking.

These items are comprehensive enough to cover most eventualities, are mainly easily transportable and can, with certain obvious exceptions as to size or value, be kept permanently in a small box or tool box in the boot of the car. Lastly, it will be found to be of great help if a copy of the estate agent's particulars of the property can be obtained for use in preparing the report. Reference in the report to rooms as described in the particulars will assist the purchaser to follow the text more easily, and will indicate to the surveyor the extent of the property.

Preliminaries, attendance and specialists

Time is money – organisation can reduce the time needed to get the investigation under way, obtain the necessary information and prepare the report. Most surveyors evolve a personal method of approach to keep time expenditure to a minimum without sacrificing thoroughness.

Purchasers are a distraction during the investigation. It is best if the surveyor carries out his inspection and after submitting his report arranges to discuss the implications with the client – on site if required.

Quoting a fixed fee for a survey usually requires a preliminary visit – this will enable the extent of specialist attendance to be assessed. Experience is needed to decide how long the inspection will take – long inspections are likely to need a commensurate time to be expended on the preparation of the report. The cost of this preliminary visit needs to be built into the fee but the client may well save money in the long run as the whole operation will be more tightly controlled.

'Attendance' is the service provided by a builder or technical specialist to assist the surveyor in carrying out his inspection and preparing his report. A builder may be employed to carry out drain tests, make available ladders, and help the surveyor to inspect areas of the building inaccessible by any other means.

'Technical specialists' are experienced and often professionally qualified individuals employed to test and give an opinion on the condition and efficiency of specific installations and equipment. Builders usually charge for their services on a 'daywork' basis – technical specialists on a fee basis.

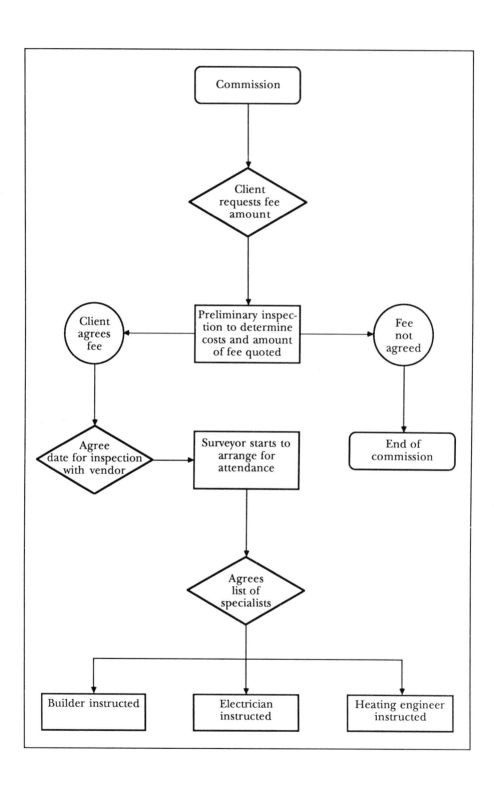

It is quite in order for the surveyor to request both to quote him a fixed charge for their work if he is asked to quote a fixed fee.

Technical specialists employed in domestic building surveys generally comprise:

○ Electrical engineers to report on the wiring, electrical equipment and electric heating installation if provided.
○ Mechanical installations engineers to report on heating plant and equipment.
○ Structural engineers where known structural defects are in evidence.
○ Lift engineers where, as in so many properties, a lift is installed.
○ Specialist woodworm and rising damp surveyors in property where such problems are known or are likely to exist.

Any serious problems that come to light during the inspection, and on which specialist opinion is required, should be brought to the purchaser's notice and his instructions should be obtained.

A date for the survey must be fixed with the vendor or his agent, convenient to all taking part, and the date and time of the inspection should be confirmed in writing to:

○ The vendor.
○ The purchaser,
○ and all providing attendance.

Prompt attendance on site is required from the builder so that he can immediately erect ladders and open up manholes ready for the surveyor. His duties must be clearly defined by the surveyor and include:

○ Provision of suitable ladders to reach the areas to be inspected.
○ Provision of short ladder for internal roof access when a loft ladder is not installed.
○ Provision of suitable equipment for drain tests (see p. 93).

Sufficient labour should be provided to raise and fix ladders and to steady them when in use.

Technical specialists also need direction from the surveyor to ensure that their opinions cover matters on which he needs guidance.

Electrical engineers should be provided with:

○ Information regarding any specialist equipment within the building to be tested.

○ Information regarding any specialist electric heating to be tested, e.g., underfloor heating circuits.
○ Request for the engineer to test and advise on the adequacy of the main intake cable and fuseways for any extension to the loading.

Mechanical installations engineers should be provided with:
○ Details of type of heating installation.
○ Fuel employed.
○ Full requirements of the purchaser in connection with the adequacy or otherwise of the existing installation.
○ A request for a firm specification and estimate for upgrading the installation if required.
○ A request for a report on the adequacy of the existing flue in respect of size and construction in connection with the fuel used or proposed and the loading of the installation boiler.

Lift service engineers should be provided with:
○ Details of the manufacturer, size and type of lift to be inspected.
○ Request for an opinion on the standard of operating machinery and ropes.
○ Request for details of the safety of the installation as inspected and a specification and estimate for upgrading the installation as required to meet operating and safety regulations.

Specialist reports are best dealt with as Appendixes to the main report (see p. 125) or, if not received before the main report is issued, as a Supplementary Report, accompanied by a covering letter summarising the conclusions reached. The surveyor should arrange to collect keys to all empty properties (unless these are brought to site by the agents where the property is furnished but unoccupied). Keys, if borrowed, should be returned to the agents immediately after the inspection has been completed.

Initial procedure on site

Brief details of the building to be inspected are usually given to the surveyor with his instructions. From these details he will be able to determine whether a preliminary visit to site is necessary to establish what attendance is required and the complexity of the problem. As mentioned before, most clients ask for a budget fee to be quoted for the work and it is difficult to do this with any precision unless the site and work involved have been properly evaluated.

If no preliminary visit has been made, the surveyor must allow himself sufficient time to familiarise himself with the layout of the property before builder and specialists arrive. To avoid any delay in commencing the inspection he must immediately on arrival carry out the following tasks to enable him to give precise and proper directions:

○ Make himself known to the occupier if the property is in occupation or open up the premises if vacant.

○ Locate the general run of drains, check the positions of manholes and decide on the scope and method of testing.

○ Locate main service entry positions and controls.

○ Carry out a quick inspection of the property to locate roof access traps and method of entry.

○ Note any portions of the structure where assistance in gaining entry is required.

○ Decide where ladders are to be positioned to gain access to valley gutters, flat roofs and such portions of the structure that are potentially defective.

○ Ensure that access to the property is clear and that parked vehicles will not cause a hazard to traffic.

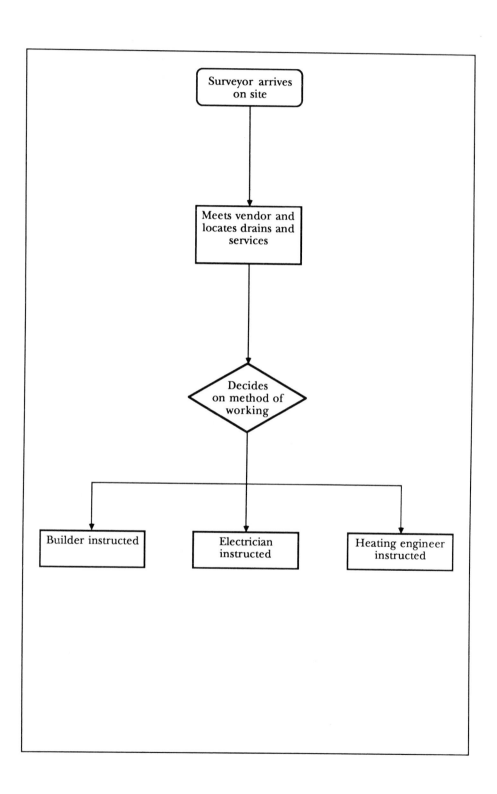

Time is money. The surveyor must ensure that he meet the builder and each specialist immediately on arrival on site to issue such instructions and information necessary to enable them to commence their work. These instructions will vary with each property, but the following may serve as a guide. The builder should be instructed to:

○ Erect ladders where required. Do not wait until you want access, the workmen will by then be involved in other tasks and delay will occur.

○ Provide access to the roof, if no built-in access ladder is fitted, and open the hatch.

○ Proceed with tests on the foul and, if required, the storm water drainage systems. Open up all manhole covers and protect openings as necessary to avoid accidents.

When using long ladders to gain access to roofs, etc., make sure they are properly tied in to the guttering or similar fixings and that a workman is stationed at the foot while the ladder is in use. Safety is paramount and no building employee would consider using ladders without such measures being in force.

The electrical specialist should be informed about:

○ The location of electrical intake and control gear.

○ The location of any specialist control gear or circuits so that these are not overlooked.

○ Any specific instructions regarding plant being left running while the inspection is being carried out.

The heating specialist should be informed about:

○ The position of the boiler and control gear.

○ Any specific instructions regarding plant being left running while the inspection is being carried out.

○ Whether testing of the boiler, electrical equipment and circuits is being carried out by the electrical specialist.

It is not necessary for the surveyor to be present for the whole time that specific tests are being carried out. He will have ensured, often from experience, that the men are fully experienced and competent in carrying out the mechanics of their trade. He will ensure, however, that he is kept informed of progress and that any irregularities or abnormalities are immediately brought to his attention.

General principles

The two basic principles to be followed in carrying out an inspection of property are:

○ To operate on the basis of a proper sequence so that each building element is inspected in its proper relationship to the building as a whole.

○ To inter-relate each element so that the cause and effect of defects can be properly recorded in such a way that the subsequent report can be prepared in a logical manner.

In order to embody these basic principles the inspection should be carried out in the same sequence of operation as is to be followed in preparing the report. This will minimise the risk of omission, economise in the time taken to carry out the inspection and subsequently to prepare the report which will follow logically from the inspection, and will reduce the physical exertion employed.

Property inspections can be physically tiring and to avoid the necessity of retracing steps, the aim of the surveyor should be to commence his inspection at the top of the building within the roof space and work his way down through the various floors leaving the drains, installations and external works to the last.

Each building will present different problems to the surveyor, but it will be found that domestic inspections can be divided into seven sections each dealing with a separate element of the building. In addition, a general description of the building must be prepared to head the subsequent report. The following list will be found suitable:

○ General description.

○ Roof.

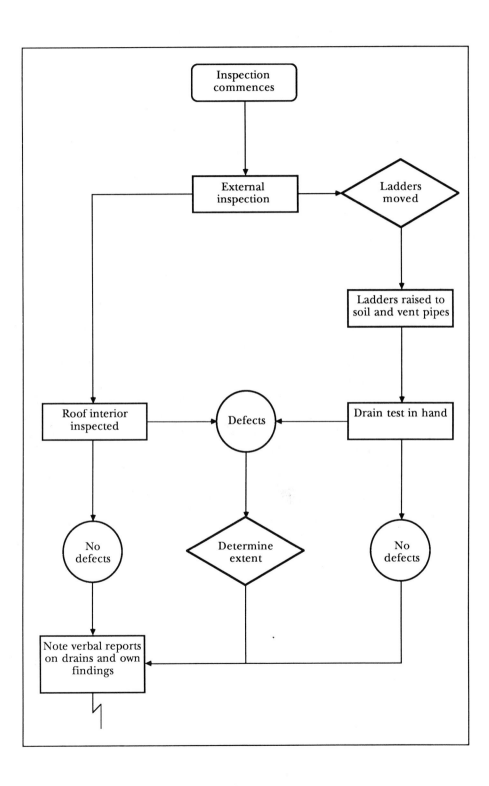

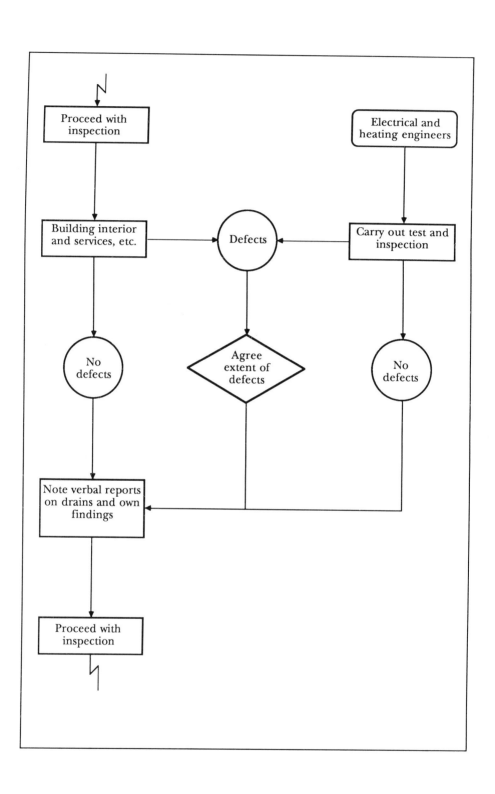

○ Walls.
○ Floors and staircases.
○ Internal finishes.
○ Drainage.
○ Services.
○ External works.
These sections, when divided and subdivided, should cover most contingencies to be encountered.

Preparation and recording of site notes

Never trust to memory – always record in writing the results of the site inspection as it is carried out.

There are a number of different methods for preparing and recording site notes:

○ By the use of a tape recorder or
○ Dictation to a secretary, both against a series of standard headings provided by an elemental check list or
○ By completing the various appropriate elements of a comprehensive check list on site as the inspection proceeds.

For a number of reasons the use of the comprehensive check list is the best method to use as it:

○ Encourages a methodical approach to the problems of the inspection.
○ Provides sufficient information for the preparation of the different formats that may be required for the presentation of the report.
○ Provides 'on the spot' confirmation of the findings of the inspection, which may be required should any portion of the report or conclusion be challenged.

The drafting of the report can be carried out by hand, by oral dictation to a secretary or by putting the report straight on to tape. The first two methods are administratively expensive and every effort should be made to become proficient in the latter method. By using a previous report as a guide to layout and sequence the risk of error or omission is reduced to a minimum.

A number of different formats are in general use:

○ The standard sequence as shown in the check lists is applicable to most situations.

○ Certain institutions, e.g., banks, which use the reports as a basis for loans to employees, etc., need a format that meets their own requirements and will supply details of these.

The check list sequence shown provides sufficient information and reference to meet all normal requirements.

Always remember that most reports are commissioned by and will be read by laymen or women who may well be confused by intricate or highly technical language. If technical terminology is unavoidable, an explanatory note should be provided so that the reader is in no doubt as to the precise meaning.

Sentences should be short and to the point and contain no ambiguous statements.

Precision and clarity are the essence of a well-written and well-presented report.

Particular attention should be paid by the surveyor to any specific matters raised by the client in connection with the property. However well the inspection is carried out, and however clear, precise and efficient the report, if the items on which specific information has been requested are ignored by the surveyor the client will justly feel aggrieved at what he will consider lack of professional attention to his requirements.

General description

The preliminaries of property purchase are often long and wearisome, but eventually vendor and a purchaser reach a point in the transaction when its outcome is dependent on the structural state of the building and any possible adjustment in the agreed value 'subject to survey'. Both parties are now anxious for the outcome, and speed in carrying out the inspection and submitting the report is crucial. The professional success of the surveyor depends largely on his ability to arrange quickly for the inspection and submission of the report.

○ The period between receipt of instructions and carrying out the inspection should not exceed two to three days.
○ The report should be submitted to the client within two days of the inspection.

While most surveyors carry out surveys in their own locality there are occasions when the property is located at some distance from the office. In such cases it should be remembered that:

○ Building methods relate to particular local materials and vary from one geological region to another.
○ The particular idiosyncrasies of individual local building surveyors and inspectors often leave a lasting impression on the buildings in their areas.
○ The nature of the subsoil can have a marked effect on the construction and performance of foundations and drains.
○ Experience that may be valid in one's own area may not be applicable in another district or county.

The report should begin with a brief general description of the property. Make this genuinely informative – not a padded version of the estate agent's particulars. The check list shows how this section of the report should be organised and prepared. The information should be set out in four separate paragraphs incorporating:

○ The age of the property and a brief description of the accommodation and its disposition.

○ The situation, aspect and location of the property and its social character.

○ The physical delineation and features of the site, frontage width and depth of plot and access.

○ The relationship of the property to neighbouring buildings and any common facilities.

Check list: How to set out a survey

The following check list has been prepared from a system that has been in use for some time. The layout of this list has evolved directly from the general principles laid down in Chapter 6 and is suitable for use in the majority of structural surveys carried out on small domestic properties. It may well be, however, that certain local peculiarities of construction are not catered for in these lists. Adjustments to provide for this contingency must be borne in mind.

Date of inspection
Address of property
Occupied/empty
Key from
Freehold/leasehold
Client's   *name*
                     address

Special instructions

General Description
Age
Accommodation
Situation
Site   *frontage*
                   depth
Access   *pedestrian*
                   vehicular

General remarks

Roof 1

Exterior description	*finish main*
	hips
	ridge
	verge
	other roofs
General condition	
Eaves	*construction*
	projection
	defects
Gutters	*materials*
	size
	condition
	adequacy
Rainwater pipes	*materials*
	size
	condition
	adequacy
Flashings, etc.	*chimneys*
	abutments
	gutters
General remarks	

Roof 2

Interior access	*construction*
	boarded areas
	condition of timbers
	infestation
Flues in roof space	
Party and/or gable walls	
Rain penetration	*generally*
	back of stacks
	valley
	flats
	torching
Insulation	
Ceiling finish	

Storage cistern   *material*   *age*

                                capacity   *condition*

                                insulation   *cover*

                                support

General remarks

Pipework   *material*

                                condition

                                insulation

General remarks

Walls 1
External finish
Condition
Pointing
Decoration
Gables
Chimney stacks
Plinth
Deflection
General remarks

Foundations   *subsoil*

                                type

                                settlement

                                defects

Air bricks   *type*   *size*

                                position

                                adequacy

                                obstructions

Damp course   *material*

                                obstructions

                                relative level (gr. fl. lev.)

                                relative level (gr. lev.)

                                rising damp

                                continuity

                                pointing

General remarks

Walls 2

Windows   *type*
                 material
                 sub-frame
                 sill
                 position in rebate
                 finish
                 condition
                 glazing   *single/double*
General remarks

Doors   *type*
                 material
                 frame
                 threshold
                 finish
                 condition
General remarks

Putty condition
Flashings materials (incl. position trays)
                 adequacy
General remarks

Balconies   *construction*
                 rail
                 finish
General remarks

Floors and staircases

Floors   *construction t. & g. yes*
                 stability   *no*
                 finish
                 deflection
                 infestation
                 defects
                 damage
                 surface condition
                 exp. joints
                 access traps
General remarks

Stairs	*construction*
	soffit open/sealed
	treads
	finish
	nosing
	condition
	ease of going
	string
	well apron
	balustrade
	stability
	infestation
	defects
	damage
General remarks	

Internal finishes
Plaster
Ceiling

Walls	*finish*
	insulation
	friezes
	roses/centres
General remarks	

Internal standard

Woodwork	*standard*
	condition
	infestation
	decorative repair
General remarks	

Decorations	*standard*
	condition
General remarks	
Fittings	

Drainage 1

Outfall	*foul*
	stormwater

Interceptor
Fresh air inlet

Manholes	*construction*
	covers
	rendering
	channels
	benching
Drains	*material*
	size
Tests	*hydraulic*
	smoke
	pneumatic

General remarks (see sketch plan)

Gullies	*material*
	description
	size
	curbs
	condition

General remarks

Drainage 2

Vent shafts	*material*
	size
	condition
	adequacy
S. & v. ps	*material*
	size
	condition
	adequacy
	system
Waste pipes	*material*
	size
	condition
	adequacy
Cesspools	*size*
	capacity
	condition
	overflow
Septic tanks	*size*
	capacity
	condition
	outfall

Adequacy of installation

Services 1
Water
Main supply
Position
Stop and drain cock
Rising main   *material*
                           position
                           condition
                           protection
Storage

Water
Cold water service   *control*
                           material
                           adequacy
General remarks

Water
Hot water service   *control*
                           storage
                           material
                           insulation
                           adequacy
General remarks

Services 2
Immersion heater
Gas circulator
Electric water heater *adequacy*
General remarks

Gas   *specialist*
                           gas board
                           verbal report
General remarks

Electrical   *specialist*
                           verbal report
General remarks

Heating fuel solid/oil/gas/electricity
Storage capacity   *solid*
                           oil

Type of installation
Open fires   *number*
                     type
                     back boiler
                     adequacy
General remarks

Boiler   *rating*
                     position
                     accelerated
Central heating   *specialist*
                     verbal report
General remarks
Flue and chimney

External works
Boundaries   *defined/undefined*
General remarks

Fences and gates   *material*
                     condition
General remarks

Grounds and garden *hedges*
                     condition
                     paths and drive
                     trees
General remarks

Outbuildings   *description*
                     condition
General remarks

Garage   *construction*
                     infestation
                     defects
                     doors
General remarks

Liability to flooding
Height above sea level
Streams wet/dry area

The roof

The inspection and report on the structural condition of the roof is divided into two distinct parts:
○ The exterior, and
○ The interior (where applicable)
These two parts are also divisible into:
○ The finishes and related elements.
○ The structure, and
○ Contained services and equipment.
The check list is therefore prepared with these divisions in mind to enable the information to be recorded in a manner that follows the progress of the inspection. As the majority of domestic properties have roofs of pitched construction the check list is prepared accordingly, but space has been allocated for other types of roof construction and finish.
The state of the roof is a good indication of the general structural stability of the building, because most serious movement in the supporting foundations and walls will be reflected in the planes of the roof weathering. Careful inspection of the profile can reveal:
○ Deflection of the ridge indicating settlement of the roof structure.
○ Loss of eaves alignment indicating spread of the roof members or loss of plumb in external walls.
○ Break in even surface of tiling or slating on either side of supporting walls indicating settlement of roof structure.
Inspection of the exterior of the roof can generally be carried out from ground level using good binoculars. Access to flat areas or areas hidden from the ground should be by ladder (see chapter 3 – attendance). A number of specific defect symptoms relating to specific roof finishes can be noted.

Tiled and slated roofs

Tiled roofs are weathered with a great variety of different profiled tiles but always manufactured from either clay or a fine concrete. Care must be taken correctly to describe the pattern used and the material from which it is manufactured. Slate roofs are generally blue/grey Welsh, but green Cumbrian can be found on good quality building of pre-war vintage. Check the size because this will affect the pitch to avoid creep. Matters to note and comment on include:

Generally
○ Ridge, hip and gable verges all sound and well pointed up in mortar.
○ Stout hip irons provided at hip ends.
○ All broken and missing units.
○ Any areas of slipping tiles or slates indicating nail sickness or rotten battens.
○ Roof slope adequate for pattern of unit used.
○ Proper double courses at eaves and verges.

Tiled roofs
○ Plain tiles manufactured with adequate camber to restrict water creep.
○ Inspect old tiled roofs for lamination.

Slate roofs
○ Check for nail sickness endemic with old slate roofs.
○ Check for lamination and/or fractures across the slate indicating poor quality material.
○ Check slate and half used at verges not slips as often found.
○ Check valleys for sound and adequate weathering with lead valleys or soakers.

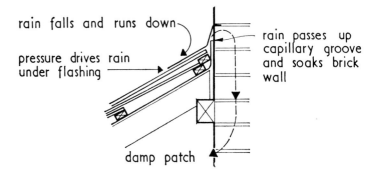

rain falls and runs down

pressure drives rain
under flashing

rain passes up
capillary groove
and soaks brick
wall

damp patch

Wind pressure drives water under flashing

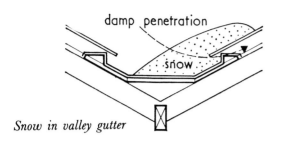

damp penetration

snow

Snow in valley gutter

Where the axis of the valley is East/West, snow melts more rapidly on the North slope, slides to bottom, packs in and provides lead for damp penetration on South side

Check List	Roofs: Tiled and slated	
Element	*Symptom*	*Defect*
Ridges and hips	Rot in ridge timbers. Rot in hip rafters. Slipping hip tiles (h.r.). Rot in hip rafters.	Missing or defective pointing. Missing hip irons. Defective lead rolls.
Eaves	Rot in fascia or soffit.	Sarking cut short of gutter. Defective vent pipe soaker. Single course at eaves. Lack of paint.
Gables	Rot in bargeboard.	Single course at verge. Defective verge pointing. Verge tiles not set properly. Use of slip tiles not tile and half. Lack of paint.
Main slopes	Missing slates or lead tingles. Loose or chattering tiles. Uneven courses or areas of slipped tiles. Surface of tiles broken. Humps over party walls. Uneven areas of flat plain tiles.	Tired or rusted nailing. Broken tiles or wrong gauge. Defective battens. Lamination. Deflection of rafters next brickwork, or battens not set properly over wall when leaking parapet to party wall pulled down below roof level. Rot in battens, caused by capillary attraction. Rot in battens, caused by old and defective torching.

Asphalt flats

Asphalt flats were rare before the 1920s and came into general
use for flat roof finishes in the immediate pre-war years. They
are generally adequate where the underlying structure is
sound, but respond badly to settlement because the material
is basically rigid and non-pliable after laying. New asphalt
is clear, bright and black and well dressed with sharp sand
and finished with asbestos cement paving tiles. With age the
surface of asphalt:
○ Becomes granular, brittle and crazed.
○ Begins to break up.
○ Cracks open up in the surface due to underlying structural movement.
○ The material cracks at points of stress such as wall
 abutments and eaves.
The inspection should take careful note of any points where
the asphalt is penetrated by:
○ Balcony railings, etc.
○ Soil and vent shafts.
○ Gullies draining stormwater from the roof surface.

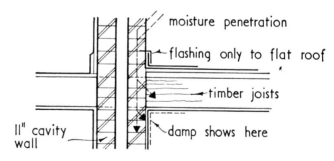

Junction of flat roof with main wall

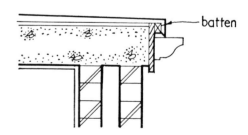

Asphalt flats
Batten at eaves and top of fascia liable to wet rot.
Surface crazing and fissuring indicate renovation or renewal.
Look for crack at eaves and angles due to uneven movement.

Check List		Roofs: Asphalt flats
Element	*Symptom*	*Defect*
Verges	Rot in fascia.	Defective weather check. No undercut bottom edge. Crack in asphalt due to thermal movement.
Upstands and Abutments	Damp on ceiling below or in adjacent wall.	Crack in angle. Top edge not weathered. Top edge not turned into brick joint. Defective flashing. Not sufficient upstand. Capillary action under flashing.
Corners	Split in asphalt.	Thermal or structural stress in old asphalt.
Surfaces	Granular.	Old asphalt in good order if no sign of damp below.
	Crumbles.	Old asphalt nearing the end of its life.
	Cracked on surface.	Old asphalt in need of renewal.
Pavings (a/c)	Loose or cracked tiles.	Bedded hollow or in poor bitumen. Insufficient bedding bitumen.
Outlets	Damp in structure below.	Asphalt not dressed properly to luting flange. Fitting not provided with luting flange.
	No grating.	Possible restriction or blockage in pipe at bottom bend.

Asphalt should be dressed at least 150mm vertically up any penetrating element and properly sealed to same.

Gullies should have proper luting flanges and the asphalt should be properly dressed into and sealed to the iron.

Abutments should have the asphalt dressed vertically 150mm with top edge dressed into a horizontal joint with the top edge weathered and a bold angle fillet provided at the junction of roof and vertical asphalt.

Lead flat roofs, etc.

All metal weathered roofs have a basic problem – the relatively high coefficient of thermal expansion. This requires the metal to be laid in small areas with thermal movement joints at sides and ends. As most supporting decking is of timber construction the jointing of the metal sheets must be adequate to prevent water penetration with consequential rotting of the substructure timbers.

Jointing is generally carried out in one of two methods:
○ Seam welts, which should be double lapped with fixing clips at intervals not exceeding 600mm, or
○ Rolls, where the undercut to resist capillary attraction must be adequate.

It is usual to use softwood boarding as a supporting decking and this should be provided with an interleaving layer of building paper, or there will be a possibility of electrolytic action between the lead sheathing and ferrous nail heads. Gutters and abutments to the building structure are general points of weakness and likely water penetration. Proper use of clips will keep the metal tight against the structure. Face nailing through the metal with copper nails is unsatisfactory – a proper welted finish will stop water penetration through the holes into the fascia.

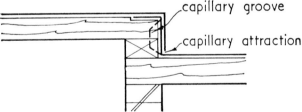

Detail of drip in lead flat to avoid capillary attraction and consequent wet rot.
Capillary groove should be provided as shown by broken line.

Bituminous felt roofs

These roofs must always be classed as 'temporary' because their usual lifespan is rarely more than 10 years before total replacement. There is a wide variety of different grades with only one common factor that they are manufactured by the impregnation of natural or mineral fibres in a bituminous compound. The upper layer as fixed can be either plain or as manufactured with an integral coloured granular exposed

Check List		Roofs: Lead flats
Element	*Symptom*	*Defect*
Verge	Rot in fascia.	Capillary attraction under welt. Water penetration through close nailing.
Upstands and Abutments	Damp on ceiling below or in adjacent wall.	Crack in angle. Defective flashing or tray. Insufficient upstand. Capillary attraction under flashing.
Seams	Damp on ceilings below. Rot in supporting boards, indicated by soft spot.	Split in lead. Seams not properly formed. Capillary attraction.
Rolls	ditto	Split in lead. Capillary attraction. Rolls not properly formed. Electrolytic action from nail heads.
Gutters	ditto	Split in lead. Capillary attraction. Electrolytic action from nail heads.
Surfaces	ditto	Split in lead. Electrolytic action from nail heads.
	Board marks on surface.	Absence of felt or building paper under lead.
	Small holes in surface.	Electrolytic action from nail heads.
	Wet patch on side cheeks of dormers or any vertical surface lined with lead.	Defective lead dot.

Note: Defects and symptoms in copper and zinc roofs are in the main similar to lead where applicable.

surface or, as now required by the Building Regulations, by chipping finish applied over a dressing of bitumen to act as a thermal reflective.

It is generally impossible from inspection of the upper surface to discover the precise number of layers of felt applied to the roof decking. Because felt roofs are subject to thermal stresses in a similar manner to metal roofs, and being weaker in tension tend to tear along stress lines, the inspection should concentrate where these are likely to occur:

○ At changes of direction of the supporting structure.
○ At ridges, verges, eaves and abutments.
○ At rainwater outlets and where vent pipes pass through the roof around roof lights.

In most cases, defective bituminous felt roofing systems will show as water penetration into the building below, either as:

○ Damp areas on the ceilings, or
○ As bitumen staining along the construction joints in the soffits of concrete ducking slabs.

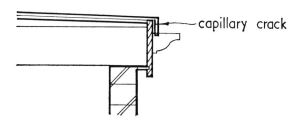

Bituminous felt roofing
Capillary crack causes rot in unpainted portion of fascia under welt (also found in lead flats).
Look for expansion cracks in width of felt, lifting on badly sealed laps and damaged bubbles.

Check List	Roofs: Bituminous felt	
Element	*Symptom*	*Defect*
Ridges	Rot in ridge board.	Defective joint or split in material. Insufficient lap.
Eaves	Rot in fascia.	Felt cut short of gutters. Capillary attraction under close welt.
Verges	Rot in bargeboard.	Capillary attraction under welt. Defective joint in metal verge flashing. Defective joint between felt and metal verge flashing.
Upstands and Abutments	Damp on ceiling below or adjacent wall.	Crack in angle. Top edge not protected by flashing or tray. Insufficient upstand. Capillary attraction under flashing.
Surface	Bubble on surface. Damp patch on ceiling.	Water vapour trapped under felt, check for damage. Stress crack in felt or defective seam joint. Heavy traffic on chippings causing perforation of felt.
Outlets	Damp in structure below. No grating.	Felt not dressed properly to flange of outlet. Defective joint of outlet to rwp. Possible restriction or blockage in pipe at bottom bend.

Roof components

The various components of the roof structure should be inspected with a view to commenting on their design and performance in the report.

Eaves design and construction follow aesthetic trends in good quality building. Their function is simply to:

○ Keep stormwater collected from the roof away from the underlying building structure.

○ Allow for the suitable support of gutters and fall pipes to ensure speedy removal of the stormwater, and

○ Protect the face of the building below from stormwater falling as rain.

Many building designers fail to appreciate these basic requirements and their buildings show, by the early onset of surface deterioration, how destructive such lack of appreciation can be.

Parapets were often of solid brick construction and the problems of weathering are rarely solved or satisfactory. The bond used on brick parapet walls will indicate whether solid or cavity. Carrying the roof finish through the wall by means of a metal tray will materially affect the strength and stability of the structure. Often this damp proof membrane was omitted resulting in:

○ Damp penetration into the underlying external walls.

○ Rot in the joist and rafter ends and supporting wall plate.

Sometimes the back face of the parapet wall is rendered, always a sign that the construction is defective.

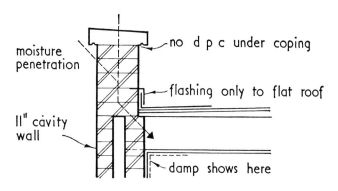

Junction of solid parapet wall with flat roof.

Check List		Roofs: Eaves and parapets
Element	*Symptom*	*Defect*
Fascia	Out of line.	Settlement of roof timbers, or rotation of supporting walls.
	Rot showing through paint film.	Sarking felt not carried over fascia into gutter. No primer on back. Cut edges at joints not reprimed before fixing.
Soffit	Rot showing through paint film.	Faulty s + vp soaker flange. Sarking felt not carried over fascia into gutter.
Flush eaves	Rot showing through paint film.	No back priming. Cut joints and mitres not reprimed. Timbers fixed direct to wall without air space. Defective capping at junction of flat roof and eaves.
Parapets	Bricks blowing on face.	Frost damage in saturated solid parapet wall.
	Defective pointing.	Ditto.
	Damp stains on ceiling below.	No horizontal dpc. Back gutter defective. Cavity tray missing or defective. RW outlet defective.

Rainwater pipes and gutters

Effective collection and disposal of stormwater falling on to roofs is essential to the well-being of the underlying structure. While gutters need not be designed to cope with exceptional rainstorms, which occur with relative infrequency, they must be able to cope with all normal downpours. Gutters must be of adequate capacity, set to proper falls to outlets and these should be situated in such positions and the rainwater pipes provided be of adequate bore to remove and

discharge the water into the drainage system provided.
Gutters should be checked from the ladders to see that:
○ The interiors are free from organic deposits and rust.
○ All surfaces are well painted.
○ All gutter joints are sound and watertight.
○ Gutter brackets to half round gutters are provided at not more than 1 metre centres.
○ Ogee pattern gutters are securely screwed to the fascia.
○ Sarking felt where provided is properly dressed into the gutter.
Rainwater pipes should be checked to see that:
○ They are securely fixed to the structure at centres not exceeding 2 metres.
○ All surfaces are adequately painted including the backs next to the wall.
○ There are no rust holes or broken sections.
○ The joints in pipes discharging direct and sealed into drains without gullies are left loose fit.
Internal valley gutters in pitched roofs are often a source of trouble – rarely inspected until defects and water penetration occurs. Typical problems which can occur are:
○ Blocked down pipes causing excessive build-up of water overflowing gutter.
○ Melting snow build up causing capillary attraction to induce water penetration into roof space.
○ Deterioration of the lead gutter sole for reasons described previously in lead flat roofs.
○ Physical damage by gutter being used as walkway for access to TV aerials, etc.

Inspection of the interior of pitched roofs should first note:
○ The location and construction of the access.
○ Details of any permanent methods of access such as loft ladders.
○ The extent of boarded storage or access areas.
○ Precise details of any roof areas where access is either difficult or impossible.
Following this the structure should be carefully inspected and its construction evaluated. No two roofs are constructed alike. At one time roofs were provided with usable space, pitches were steeper, flat apexes were sometimes provided to reduce the height on large square houses. In such buildings the

following information should be recorded:

○ The sawn sizes, spans, centres of support and methods of jointing of all timbers.

○ Rafters provided in single lengths or scarf jointed over purlins.

○ Purlins strutted at centres not exceeding 1800mm, struts notched to undersides of purlins with feet notched over longitudinal binders.

○ Ceiling joists in one piece or if jointed, joints placed centrally in span and preferably over a supporting partition.

○ Purlins may be built into gable walls but not into party walls where brick or block corbel supports should be provided.

○ Roof timbers properly trimmed around chimney stacks, etc.

Inspection of the underside of the roof slope will show if the roof is provided with sarking felt or whether the soffit is boarded. If the latter and nails protrude it is likely that the boarding is fixed reverse feather edge without battens to carry the slates or tiles.

Many houses built before 1939 have neither sarking felt nor boarded soffits. To reduce draughts, rain or snow penetration, the joints between the battens and the slates or tiles were provided with a lime mortar fillet, called 'torching'. This fillet tends to decompose with time and falls to the ceiling below. In addition the porous hygroscopic nature of the material tends to produce conditions conducive to wet rot in the battens.

Roof timbers when new are clean and bright from the saw. As they age they become dull and turn a grey colour. This characteristic enables repair work to be clearly visible in an old roof by the change in colour of the new timber. Three principal defects in structural timbers are of importance in assessing the strength and fitness of any roof component:

○ Wane, which is a loss of arris caused by faulty alignment during conversion of the original log and results in loss of cross-sectional area and consequently strength.

○ Fissures occuring naturally in the timber both with and against the grain, causing loss of strength.

○ Knots which when large and dead can cause failure of the member.

These defects should be clearly noted where they occur and

recommendations for strengthening or replacement should be made in the report.

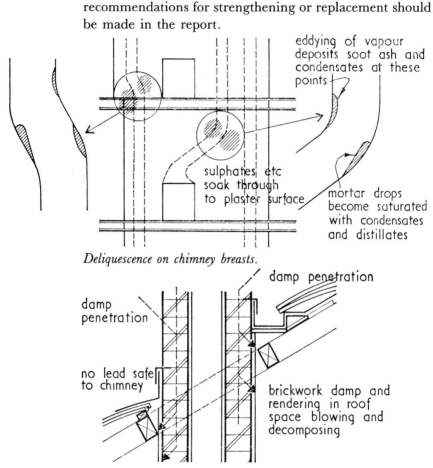

eddying of vapour deposits soot ash and condensates at these points

sulphates etc soak through to plaster surface

mortar drops become saturated with condensates and distillates

Deliquescence on chimney breasts.

damp penetration

damp penetration

no lead safe to chimney

brickwork damp and rendering in roof space blowing and decomposing

Junction of roof slope and stack with absent or faulty lead safe.

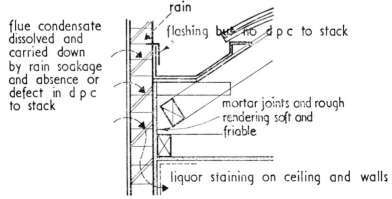

rain

flue condensate dissolved and carried down by rain soakage and absence or defect in d p c to stack

flashing but no d p c to stack

mortar joints and rough rendering soft and friable

liquor staining on ceiling and walls

Damp penetration due to omission of dpc in stack.

Internal flues

Old flues were parged either in haired lime mortar or later in cement and sand. It is only during the last decade or so that terracotta flue liners have been a requirement of the Building Regulations. In course of time the old flue linings deteriorate due to the absorption of condensed moisture and spirit vapours. This problem is more usual in flues exposed to severe weather on external walls or where the flue temperature is unsufficient to 'burn out' condensation. Externally the defect is apparent from distortion of the stack, internally in the roof space by deterioration of the rough rendering to the flue or mortar joints in exposed brickwork.

Chimney stacks

Old chimneys were often constructed without proper damp courses or, if they were provided they were fixed high above the roof line or well below the roof level. Chimneys are particularly exposed to the weather and the structure becomes saturated after heavy rain. Inspection is generally carried out from the ground by means of binoculars and from within the roof space. A number of defects and their likely cause are shown on the checklist.

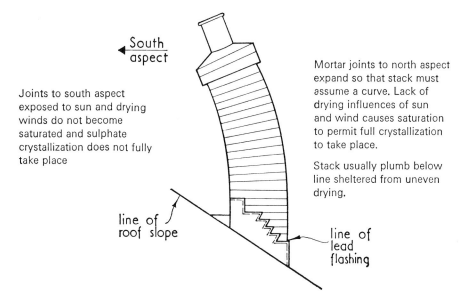

Effect of sulphate attack in domestic boiler flue.

Check List	Roofs: Chimneys	
Element	*Symptom*	*Defect*
Chimney stacks	Brickwork above roof stained and pointing defective.	Sulphate attack.
	Stack leans south.	ditto
	Dark stains on ceiling next to chimney breast.	ditto
	Rough rendering in roof space soft and blown.	ditto
	Mortar joint in roof space and externally soft and friable.	ditto
	Brickwork below roof line wet.	Defective or missing safe, flashings, back gutter or soaker, depending on position.
	Black stains on chimney breast and plaster in rooms.	Faulty parging allowing deposition of soot against porous brickwork and consequent penetration of sulphate liquor.
	Cracks in chimney capping.	Probably caused by old fire in flue.
	Cracks in rough rendering	In isolated stacks probably due to movement in flue structure.

Party walls in semi-detached or terrace houses act as compartment walls and as such are required to provide at least one hour fire resistance. This degree of fire resistance is usually provided by a 225mm wall of brick or block which also provides the statutory requirement in respect of airborne sound reduction. Party walls are generally found to be of two types:
○ Those provided up to about 1890, in which the wall was carried up above the roof slope.
○ Those which are constructed tight up to the underside of the slates or tiles.
The first type of wall has caused so many problems with water penetration that most have been pulled down below the roof

Check List		Roofs: General
Element	*Symptom*	*Defect*
Party walls	A – where these project above the roof line. Brickwork wet.	Defective soakers, flashings or cement and sand listings. Defective rendering to exposed work above roof line. Omission of dpc under brick on edge course or defective dpc.
	B – where party walls terminate under the roof covering. Brickwork wet.	Defective making out over wall where the projecting portion was removed, usually caused by the use of slate slips instead of full width slates (or tiles) or slate and half. Cocking up of tiles or slates over the party wall. Rafters or trimmers wrongly set, defective or non-existent, with consequent deformation of the roof line, caused by excessive weight on the battens.

surface and the roofing made out over the top. Such work is readily visible from outside the building. Care must be taken to see that no timbers are built into or through party walls, but if they are present it should be recommended that the free ends be properly protected by an approved fire-resisting covering.

Insulation and ceiling finish

The high cost of fuel and increasingly stringent government regulations have drawn attention to the importance of insulating the fabric of domestic buildings. While new construction generally complies with high insulation standards, older properties often fall well behind minimum requirements and the report should draw attention to any deficiencies. While inspecting the roof insulation, or lack of it, a note should be made of the method of ceiling construction. This

will be one of three types:
- Timber lath and plaster construction in pre-war properties.
- Plaster wall board in 2400 × 1200mm (approx) sheets finished with a neat plaster skin coat in low grade properties.
- Plaster lath in 1200 × 400mm (approx) sizes finished with plaster skin coat in better quality work.

Care must be taken to ensure that all ceilings are soundly fixed to supporting timbers and all movement or excessive shrinkage cracks should be recorded.

Infestation

One of the big question marks in the mind of the prospective purchaser will be 'woodworm'. In fact, it may well be his prime reason for the survey. Happily, the evidence for infestation in roof spaces (see pp. 47-49) is not hard to identify except where torching has been applied to the battens and the disintegrated material covers the ceiling joists and boarded areas with a fine powder not dissimilar to the frass from wormholes.

Apart from this the location of flight holes and their attendant dribbles of sawdust or frass is not a difficult task – the holes being generally located in the sides or soffits of timbers, sometimes in the tops and, where serious infestation occurs, in the sawn ends. A heavy concentration of active holes will indicate a serious weakening of timber strength, resulting in replacement of the scantling.

Most infestation is caused by:
- Common furniture beetle, found in the sapwood of soft woods, in all areas.
- House longhorn beetle in restricted areas in Surrey, Berkshire and parts of Hampshire.
- Powderpost beetle in the sapwood of certain hardwoods with a high sugar content.
- Death-watch beetle in oak and certain other hardwoods exposed to conditions which give rise to fungal attack.

All infestation should be treated by a specialist to eradicate present and prevent future infestation. Where treatment has been carried out prior to the inspection a copy of the guarantee should be requested to check the extent of the work and the conditions of the guarantee.

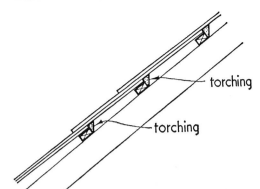

Pre-1939 slate and tile roofs without sarking felt were pointed or 'torched' to keep out wind and rain. This falls out in time, causing dirty roof and rain and snow penetration.

Torching in cheap roofs.

Common furniture beetle

Death-watch beetle

Powder post-beetle (Lyctus)

House longhorn beetle (Hylotrupes bajulus)

Check list	Roofs: General	
Element	*Symptom*	*Defect*
Infestation	Holes 1.6mm (1/16in) diam in structural timbers, plywood and joinery, associated with small quantities of fine sawdust.	Anobium punctatum (Common furniture beetle)
	Holes 3.25mm (1/8in) diam in hardwoods (usually damp) with clean walls and small quantities of fine sawdust.	Xestobium rufovillosum (Death-watch beetle)
	Holes 1.6mm (1/16in) diam in sapwood of certain hardwoods with associated fine sawdust.	Lyctus (Powderpost beetle)
	Oval holes 6mm × 10mm (1/4in × 1/3in) in softwoods with associated pellets mixed with fine sawdust. Restricted districts.	Hylotrupes bajulus (House longhorn beetle)

Plumbing within the roof space

Where water company regulations require it, water storage cisterns are usually to be found in roof spaces to ensure sufficient head of water for apparatus situated on the floor below. Sometimes these cisterns are raised on timber platforms or stillages where high level w.c. cisterns have been installed. Storage cisterns are to be found constructed of four different materials:

○ Galvanised steel, prone to corrosion in certain water areas especially around holes for pipe connections. Sometimes a cistern is finished internally with a bitumen-based corrosion inhibitor but this is rarely of much use.

○ Asbestos cement which is heavy and inflexible but immune to corrosion.

○ Fibreglass which requires to be set on a rigid supporting platform to sustain the weight of enclosed water.

○ PVC which is flexible, non-corrosive but, again, requires a rigid platform to support its weight.

The size of the cistern should be checked to ensure that it is of a capacity to hold one day's supply or 272 litres (60 gallons). Large domestic properties should have a proportionally larger supply. The ball valve should be checked for size and action and its condition recorded.

The pipework in the roof space should be inspected for:
○ Material composition and bore.
○ Sufficiency of lagging.
○ Situation in respect of possible exposure to frost damage.

Where different materials are used for storage and distribution pipework, any likelihood of electrolytic action should be investigated.

The walls

The walls of domestic properties generally serve three purposes:
○ To support the roof and intermediate floors, and
○ To provide a weatherproof envelope to protect the contents and inhabitants, and
○ To provide a degree of thermal resistance which will ensure reasonable comfort to the occupants under optimum external temperature ranges.

Failure of either of the first two would render the other defective. Low thermal resistance would produce an internal micro-climate which would be unsatisfactory. Structural failure or defects are generally indicated by movement cracks or loss of plane in the external face of the wall. Weathering defects are generally apparent by damp appearing on the inner face of the wall.

The inspection of external walls should follow the general rule of starting at the top and working down to ground level. In general, defects occur where:
○ There is a change of material or direction of the structure, or
○ Where an opening or feature breaks the continuity of the structure, or
○ Where thrust or pressure is exerted on the wall structure, usually by a point load, in excess of the capability of the wall to contain it.
○ Where the loading on the wall exceeds the bearing capacity of the subsoil, causing subsidence or excessive settling of the wall structure.

The inspection should commence with the external face,

noting such matters as may well produce internal defects. As the majority of domestic properties are constructed of brick and blockwork the check list has been prepared to suit this construction, but in areas where stone facing predominates this needs to be adjusted. Where brick facing is found the recording of defects is a relatively simple affair. Where other external finishes are found these must be considered in addition to likely defects in the substrata.

Rendered surfaces

Rendering is found on all qualities of domestic work and on both solid and cavity walls. Properly prepared and applied it provides a sound, weatherproof finish. Generally, good quality rendering can be judged by:

○ Its surface, which should be slightly roughened with an open texture.

○ Free from surface cracking or crazing which indicates usually the use of too strong a mortar mix.

○ Horizontal cracking which usually indicates thermal movement in the substrata and leads to water penetration into the wall structure.

○ The presence or otherwise of hollow or loose bonded areas where the rendering has lost bond with its backing wall.

Properties built before 1900 with externally rendered walls are usually constructed of one or one and a half brick walls. The rendering is generally about 25mm thick and internally the walls are of two or three coat plaster on timber laths fixed to battens nailed to the inner face of the external wall. This gives an overall thickness of about 300mm for one brick or 412mm for the thicker wall. Cavity walls have the plaster laid directly on to the inner face of the wall, producing a 'solid' sound when tapped in contrast to the 'hollow' sound from the plastered solid wall.

Tile hanging

Tile hanging is a popular feature in domestic work and certain counties, where clay tiles have been manufactured for centuries, a standard form of external facing. As the tile is virtually waterproof care must be taken to see that stormwater running down the external face is discharged in such a manner as to ensure that it is thrown clear of the wall

surface below, by the use of:
- Tile creased or brick corbel courses, or
- The provision of a timber tilter fillet over the heads of bay windows and similar timber constructions.

Good quality tile hanging has:
- No missing or broken tiles.
- Bottom edges formed with double tile course.
- Tile and half used to make out against vertical abutments.
- Lead soakers or a stepped flashing to weather joints against vertical abutments.
- Junctions of tile hanging and roof slopes made with lead soakers.
- External angles made with proper angle tiles or the tiles neatly cut and provided with a lead soaker under each intersecting pair of tiles.

Modern tiles have nibs which support the tiles on the batten with a single nail through the hole provided into the supporting batten. Poor quality work often has the backing brickwork laid in rat trap bond and the tiles nailed into the bedding joints which are at 112mm centres. Usually these tiles are bedded in mortar to the wall to help 'stick' them into position.

Slate hanging which is a feature of many domestic properties in areas where slates were once produced in large quantities such as Cornwall, Devon, North Wales and Cumbria, have similar defects and standards as tile hanging.

Weatherboarding

Originally restricted to areas of the country where:
- A shipbuilding tradition was firmly established, and
- Where oak suitable for riving into feather-edge boarding was abundantly available.

This facing material has now become a standard 'feature' facing material throughout the country. Modern weatherboarding is generally:
- Softwood machined to a shiplap conformation, and
- Treated with a preservative stain or painted.

Good quality work should be:
- Machined from 25mm thick material.
- Fixed to timber battens secured to the wall to provide an air space.
- The wall surface protected by a sheet of breather pattern

building paper.
○ The battens and boarding pressure treated with preservative, and
○ The backs and cut ends of the boarding treated with stain or primer before the boards are fixed.
○ Abutments provided with lead stepped flashings.
In general defects in weatherboarding are caused by:
○ Lack of preservative treatment.
○ Corrosion of ferrous fixing nails causing breakdown of paint film, water penetration and rot.
○ Water penetration into untreated cut ends causing rot.
○ Lack of primer or preservative paint seal at back allowing moisture penetration and consequential rot.
Defects in weatherboarding are generally clearly visible especially where the surface is painted, where breakdown of the paint film by underlying rotten timber can easily be seen. This is generally apparent at butt joints, mitred corners and free ends.

Brick facing work

Brick walls are composed of two different materials each with varying physical and chemical characteristics:
○ The brick itself which carries the load and protects the building from the aggressive external environment, and
○ The bedding and pointing mortar which acts as a binder to integrate the bricks into a homogenous whole and also acts as a safety valve to remove excessive water penetrating into the wall in wet weather and as a path for movement cracking.
Defects in brick walls fall into a number of clearly defined categories:
○ Use of mortar mix not suitable for its location or type of bricks used in the wall.
○ Selection of brick unsuitable by reason of strength or chemical characteristics for the use, or exposure in particular situations.
○ Excessive thrust from the structure or its use, or settlement in the foundations resulting in rotation of the wall due to thrust, or shear cracking due to uneven settlement.
○ Vertical cracking through the wall due to excess thermal or moisture movement.

In addition, in certain subsoils defects can occur due to environmental causes unrelated to the construction of the wall itself:

○ The provision of shallow foundations in clay subsoils exposing foundations and overlying wall structure to upward thrust of expanding clay in wet weather and subsequent settlement when the clay dries out in warm dry conditions.

○ The growth of trees and large shrubs adjacent to buildings within reach of the root system which, extracting water from under the building, will cause settlement of the building to fill the void created by the shrinking subsoil.

○ The provision of subsoil drainage in granular subsoils which, removing ground water flowing or static from under the wall foundations, causes settlement.

Structural cracking in external walls generally conform to the following:

○ Vertical fractures with cracks of even width from top to bottom indicate thermal or moisture movement in the wall.

○ Cracks wider at the top than at the bottom indicate that the foundation has settled to one side.

○ Cracks wider at the bottom than at the top indicate settlement under the crack and that the building has possibly broken its back.

○ Where the crack occurs in the position of maximum weakness of a wall, i.e., at window openings, and a large open crack occurs at sill level, this indicates soil heave.

○ Wide gaps or cracks occurring under exposed concrete slabs at ground level is indicative of frost heave caused by the freezing and consequent expansion of the filling or soil under the slab.

Foundations are difficult to assess unless opened up for inspection. Generally if the overlying structure shows no sign of any defect that could be attributed to foundation defects, a reasonable degree of foundation stability can be assumed.

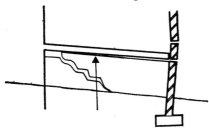

Frost damage to foundations in chalky and fine sandy soils.

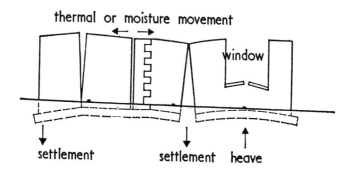

Structural defects in walls indicating difference between thermal movement and settlement and heave in foundations.

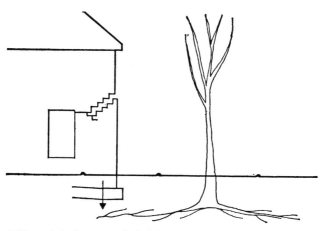

Effect of drying out of shrinkable clay by the action of tree roots.

Damp courses

Soil contains quantities of moist air. Warm air within a house rises and draws moist air out of the ground on which it is constructed. To counteract this it is a requirement that the earth under a building be covered with a damp-resistant material such as concrete either as a support for timber ground floor construction or to carry the floor finish directly. Where subsoil conditions are excessively wet a damp-proof membrane should also be provided.

Timber ground floor construction incorporates a number of basic requirements to reduce the risk of fungal attack from ground moisture:

○ A free air space of not less than 150mm between the surface of the concrete and the underside of the floor joists.

○ This space must be freely ventilated to the open air by means of air bricks not less than 215 × 65mm overall set at about 1800mm centres.

○ Air bricks should be placed preferably in the course of brickwork immediately under the damp course.

○ Air bricks should not be blocked up or covered by flower beds or paving.

Solid ground floor construction should have the top of the slab set at the level of the damp course in the external wall with floor screed and finish rising above this level. This will enable a proper junction to be made between the damp-proof membrane laid over the slab to marry up and be continuous with the damp-proof course in the wall.

Moisture rises into walls from the ground by capillary attraction through pores in the brick structure. This is prevented by the insertion through the whole thickness of the wall or its component leaves of a damp-proof course formed from either:

○ A bituminous felt strip formed from a number of binding materials impregnated with bitumen which is usual in modern properties.

○ A strip of lead protected against corrosion from the bedding cement mortar by a coating of bitumen; may be found in good quality buildings.

○ Two courses of slate laid breaking joint in cement mortar of a total visible thickness of 25mm; found in buildings usually constructed before about 1914.

Defects in damp-proof courses can cause rising damp in the overlying wall and floor structures. The defects are caused by:

○ Obstructing the damp course by flower beds, rockeries and pavings. A minimum of 150mm must be observed between damp-proof course and the surrounding ground or paved surfaces.

○ Obstructing the damp course by rendered plinths or general wall rendering which cause bridging and water penetration into the overlying wall structure.

○ Settlement of the building causing fracturing or tearing of the damp-proof course and a passage for water penetration.

○ Failure to ensure proper lapping of the damp-proof course

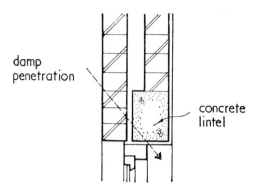

damp penetration

concrete lintel

Damp penetration over window or door opening due to faulty or missing tray.

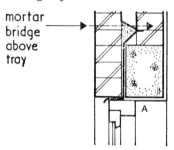

mortar bridge above tray

A

Damp penetration over window or door opening due to mortar bridge.
Note damp in corners in position 'A' usually due to tray not being carried sufficiently proud of the lintel or deformed at this point.

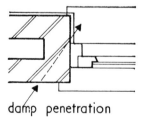

damp penetration

Damp penetration due to missing or defective vertical dpc to reveal wet rot in frames.

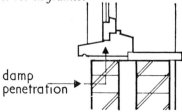

damp penetration

Damp penetration due to omission of dpc under sill causes wet rot in sill and window board.

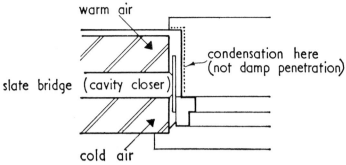

Damp penetration around window and door openings.

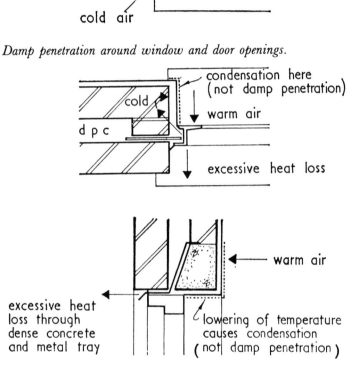

Condensation around widow and door openings.

Check List	Walls 1	
Element	*Symptom*	*Defect*
Parapets and garden walls (rendered)	Horizontal cracking in rendering following joints in structure.	Probably sulphate attack due to wrong mix. If crack is found near point of restraint the crack could be structural.
Chimneys	Crack in flue wider at top than bottom.	Probably due to fire in flue.
Eaves	Horizontal cracks to eaves of flat concrete roof.	Thermal movement.

structure due to the prevalent forms of construction adopted, and

○ Because it is easier to inspect them individually at the same time as the wall surface and construction.

Windows and doors should be described as to type, construction and material, surround, effectiveness of sill and weathering satisfaction. Good points leading to effective weather protection are:

○ Competent and suitable surface decoration.

○ Proper projection of window sills over wall surface below.

○ Provision of an adequate throating to the underside of the sill.

○ Adequate pointing to seal joint between frame and wall reveal.

○ Metal windows set back 112mm into reveal to enable vertical damp course to be properly set into rebate in back of frame.

○ Putty sound, complete and uncracked with junction of putty and glass properly sealed with paint film.

○ Sills bedded on horizontal damp course visible on external wall surface.

Decay in timber windows and doors is, despite treatment of the timber, a growing problem. Unless the window components are vacuum treated after machining and immediately before assembly rot will occur when water enters through exposed end grain. Modern glues tend to fracture under thermal stress in the timbers and, being rigid and consequently unable to take up shrinkage in the timber, allow water penetration into untreated end grain of components. This is generally found:

○ In the tenons of side members and mullions of frames at sill level often due to the omission of a damp-proof course under the sill.

○ In the ends of bottom and lock rails at their junction with sash and door stiles.

○ In the ends of softwood sills trimmed to suit brick reveals.

This defect is generally of the wet rot variety and its extent can be determined by careful prodding with a bradawl.

Damp stains around door and window openings on the plaster surface may be due to:

○ Defective vertical damp course.

○ Bridging of the cavity or damp course by mortar droppings.
○ Defective tray to the head of the opening, usually indicated by damp patches at the top corners of the opening.
○ Damp patches about 225 to 300mm above the window head indicate bridging of the cavity above the cavity tray.
○ Damp patches at sill level indicating the vertical damp-proof course cut short above the top of the built-in timber window or door sill.

Care must be taken to differentiate between damp penetration and condensation stains. At sill level the latter are generally elongated and rise above the window board from back of sill to external corner of the reveal. Cold bridging across cavities from steel lintels can cause condensation on the inner surface of the wall showing, when dry, as slightly dirty or discoloured patches. Similar problems can occur with galvanised twisted wall ties and slate cavity sealing to the reveals of openings.

Metal windows manufactured in the pre-war years were rarely galvanised and older patterns must be carefully checked for rusting. Where these have been newly painted, cracked panes of glass will usually indicate rust in the rebates under the glass. Leaded lights in exposed situations usually leak due to breakdown of the 'cement' bedding between glass and lead cames.

All openings in cavity walls must be provided with an impervious membrane to prevent the passage of water through the structure at the head of the opening. In buildings with vertical sliding sash windows, these are usually set back behind the cut or rubbed brick arch carrying the external leaf to avoid making the head of the box frame segmental. Rarely is a damp-proof membrane found in such a situation.

Balconies, borrowed from Continental fashion, are a popular feature in coastal towns. Often the concrete used in their construction provides a cold bridge across the cavity, and weather problems and lax detailing often allow water through the structure. In wet weather in exposed situations the doors provided, usually domestic standard 'patio' types, leak and are excessively draughty.

at corners, junctions of one length and another or overlapping in differing courses when the ground level falls across the face of the building.

Rising damp is generally indicated by:

○ Damp stains along and immediately above the ground floor skirting level.

○ Wet rot in ground floor skirtings.

○ Excessive moisture content in floor boards adjacent to skirting, especially in bay windows.

○ Damp staining and lifting wood flooring blocks mainly around the external perimeter of the building.

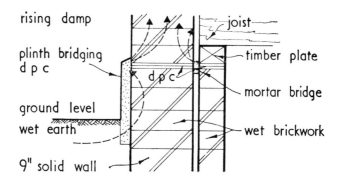

Bridging of damp courses by rendered plinth or mortar bridge.

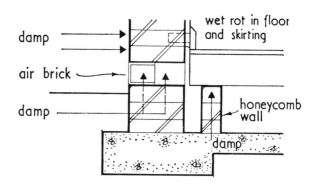

Solid wall with dpc absent or defective.

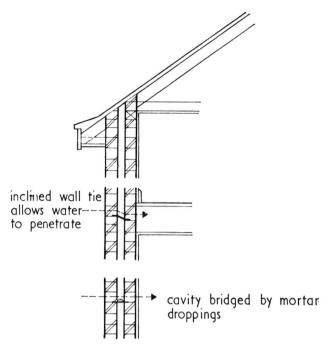

inclined wall tie
allows water
to penetrate

cavity bridged by mortar
droppings

Defects which cause damp penetration.

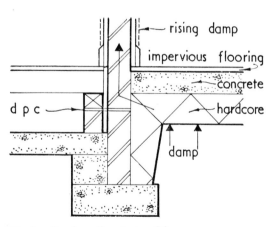

rising damp

impervious flooring

concrete

d p c

hardcore

damp

Faulty dpc insertion to partition.

Windows and doors

As we have seen, defects are more likely to occur where there
is a change of surface configuration of structural material.
Further defects can arise where openings occur in the structure. Windows and doors should be considered in conjunc-
tion with walls, being sub-elements of a primary structural
element:

○ Because their inclusion leads to possible defects in the

Check List		Walls 2
Element	*Symptom*	*Defect*
General surfaces	'Map pattern' cracking over rendered surface.	Mix too strong.
	Circular bulge with peripheral or radiating cracking of rendering.	Rendering detached and free from backing.
	Surface of rendering defaced with soft powdery excescences.	Efflorescence.
	Tile hanging missing in quantity.	Rot in battens or rusting of nails.
	Odd tile missing.	Breakage. Wind suction on badly fixed tile.
	Bottom edge of tile hanging uneven.	Rot in timber tilter.
	Internal damp stains to head of bay window with tile hung or rendered timber work over.	Rot in tilter probably spreading to window head or timber ashlaring.
	Rot in timber weatherboarding.	Damp rising from wall below due to omission of damp-proof membrane. Omission of throat or splay undercut to bottom edge. Lack of protection where boards abut brickwork. Poor decorative maintenance. Lack of ventilation at back. Omission or breakdown of back priming.
	Weatherboarding twisted or curled.	Boards too thin.
	Brick face eroded (stocks).	Mortar mix too dense and impermeable.
	Pointing defective and dislodged (stocks).	Usually smooth ironed in pointing dislodged by frost.
	Face of brickwork disintegrating (faced bricks).	Usually a recessed joint, where frost has blow off the face.

Check List		Walls 3
Element	*Symptom*	*Defect*
General Surfaces (cont.)	Pointing below dpc soft and crumbly.	Use of weak mortar mix instead of cement mortar.
	Surface blister or flaking of painted surface.	Moisture in the structure blowing off the decoration. Efflorescence, where salty crystals are found under blister.
	Air bricks not visible in external wall when timber suspended ground floor is provided.	Ground around house raised above air bricks.
	Rot in timber ground floor.	Omission or bad spacing of air bricks.
	Rising damp internally with rot in skirting or damp patches at floor level.	Defective dpc or mortar bridge at dpc level. Screed for tiles bridging dpc. Dpc bridged at junction of suspended timber and solid floors.
	Rot in central area of boarded ground floor or at perimeter not connected with rising damp in walls.	Omission or fault in dpc to sleeper walls.
	Damp patch on internal face of external wall.	Mortar on wall tie bridging cavity. Wall tie inclined to inner face of wall.
	Dry dirty patch on inner face of plastered external wall about 9in (230mm) diameter.	Cold bridge from cavity tie.
Plinths	Rising damp on internal walls.	Rendering bridging dpc in solid wall.
Foundations	Fracture in brickwork between two structures wider at top than bottom.	Settlement.

Timber ground floors have timber joists of smaller depth than upper floors because they are supported at midspan (or spans not exceeding 1800mm) by sleeper walls. The only variation is where the building is on a slope and the void under the floor is spanned by a floor construction similar to upper floors. Timber ground floors are more prone to fungal attacks than upper floors due to:

○ Insufficient cross ventilation of the void.
○ The presence of heating pipes, etc., which raise the temperature to the optimum for fungal germination.
○ The presence of moisture from tap penetration of the structure, rising damp through defective dpc, leaking pipework, etc.
○ Sealing in of the floor surface by vinyl sheeting, especially in areas of high humidity and warmth such as kitchens and bathrooms.

Otherwise timber ground floors are subject generally to the same structural problems as upper timber floors.

Solid ground floors are generally constructed of a layer of concrete with the finish either bedded or laid direct on to the concrete or a levelling screed. The most serious problem with these floors is that of bridging the damp-proof membrane in the floor, or the damp-proof course in the surrounding walls by:

○ Surface of levelling screed not level with the dpc in the walls.
○ Damp-proof membrane in floor not level with and sealed to dpc in walls.
○ Retention of timber levelling peg rising within the full depth of the oversite concrete.
○ Leaving a brickbat on the surface of the filling to be absorbed in the thickness of the oversite concrete.

All these will provide a bridge for rising damp which in particularly serious cases can lead to an outbreak of dry rot where the overlaying floor finish is of wood blocks. Inspect the perimeter and surface of the solid floor for:

○ Damp stains on the surface indicating rising damp.
○ Loss of adhesion in the blocks although this can be caused by shrinkage of the subfloor.
○ Arching and break up of wood block floors caused by rising damp and swelling of blocks.
○ Loose and detached vinyl tiles caused by break-down of

the bedding affected by rising damp.

○ Horizontal cracking of the surface and soft areas of rot next to the floor in timber skirtings.

Other problems which can occur with ground floor construction and finishes are:

○ Use of straight edge boarding in older properties – the joints opening up as the boards shrink and causing draughts.

○ Loss of adhesion by quarry tile floors due to shrinkage of the subfloor.

○ Damaged and/or loose boards where access has been gained for new services, etc.

○ Deterioration of polished surfaces of wood block and cork tile floor from contact with carpet underfelting.

Checking floors for fungal rot will require the surveyor to be familiar with the two main fungal rots encountered in buildings.

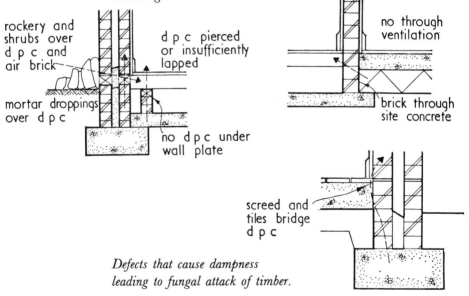

Defects that cause dampness leading to fungal attack of timber.

Dry rot (*Serpulia lacrymans*) is the most common form of fungal decay (see photo) and is caused by:

○ Poor ventilation of underfloor timbers.

○ The presence of excess moisture content in structural timbers or surrounding work, often caused by rising damp.

○ Warmth from the atmosphere or adjacent heat sources of above 18°C, although it thrives best at around 23°C.

Floors and staircases

These secondary elements of structure are the most prone to defect and can be found in a state of partial collapse due to:
○ Infestation or dry rot.
○ Wet rot due to water penetration or rising damp.
○ Excessive cutting away to accommodate and conceal electrical conduit and pipe runs.

Floors

Many floors originally adequate for the loads imposed on them are seriously weakened due to structural neglect and services alterations and additions. These are very difficult to inspect as most are covered with fitted carpets, vinyl sheeting and similar permanent or semi-permanent finishes. As the total removal of these coverings to inspect the floors in occupied premises is rarely possible, floors should be inspected in places where defects are most likely to occur:
○ Under sinks, lavatory basins and bath traps and w.c. outgoes where water can leak on to the floor unnoticed over a period.
○ In bay windows where the problems of providing a continuous dpc under the joist ends or plate can defeat the builder.
○ Around the exterior perimeter of floors butting on to solid external walls where the joist ends are either carried on or are built into the external wall.
Where the structural timber floor surface is exposed, the interior can be inspected by lifting traps left for electrical services, usually placed over the lighting point in the floor below.

Pipe runs in floors usually have floor boards over sawn out and refixed by nailing – a simple matter to lift with a strong screwdriver. Where it is not possible to inspect floors because of floor coverings this limitation should be drawn to the prospective purchaser's attention.

Buildings generally begin life plumb and level, but for a number of reasons as they age they get somewhat askew. In most properties this is virtually unnoticeable and can be discounted unless accompanied by excessive structural cracking. Floors can get out of level by:

○ Differential settlement of the structure when roof, walls and floors settle in one corner or along one side of the building.

○ Overloading of the particular floor concerned when the structure dips towards the overloaded area accompanied, on upper floors, by cracking of the underlying ceiling.

○ Excessive notching of the structural members to accomodate pipe runs and conduit, especially in the centre third of the floor span.

○ Loss of strength in the structural members due to loss of structural integrity by worm infestation or one of the fungal rots.

○ Shrinkage in the timber structure causing the wedges positioning the outside joist against the thrust of herringbone strutting to become dislodged and the floor to become 'springy'.

Upper floors have greater spans than ground floors and their structural timbers are consequently of greater depth. To check that joist depth is satisfactory, measure floor thickness at stairwell, deduct 38mm for plaster and boarding and check against formula

$$\text{depth of joist } = \left(\frac{\text{span mm}}{24} + 50 \right) \text{ mm}$$

with joists at 400mm centres. If the floor is:

○ Adequate to rule of thumb joist depth and spacing relative to span.

○ Boarding well cramped up and securely bradded down.

○ Skirting well scribed down on to the boarding around the whole perimeter of the floor.

○ Floor shows negligible vibration when subjected to percussion test.

it is likely to be structurally sound.

Check List		**Walls 4**
Element	*Symptom*	*Defect*
Foundations (cont).	Fracture of brickwork or vertical perpends of even width throughout.	Thermal or shrinkage crack.
	Stepped crack in wall from corner of building towards adjacent opening wider at top than bottom.	Settlement caused by drying out of shrinkable clay subsoil, often due to adjacent tree or shrub.
	Crack under ground floor window extending from sill into ground, sill bowed upwards.	Foundation heave in clay subsoil due to foundations being too shallow.
	Crack in wall wider at bottom than top.	Settlement under building which has tended to break its back.
	Wide crack between concrete terrace and brick retaining wall on chalk or fine sandy subsoil.	Frost heave.
Openings	Concrete lintel sags.	If no cracking, due to faulty shuttering. Cracks in soffits could mean lintel built in upside down with steel bars in top, crack usually wider at the bottom.
	Timber soffit lining is sagging (old property).	Overloaded timber lintel. Timber lintel affected by rot. (Look for damp stains on plaster from wet rot.)
	Steel angle over window head is sagging.	Overloaded. Rusting affecting strength. (Look for settlement crack in brickwork over.)
	Damp patch over head of opening.	Defect in lead tray over (central damp patch). Tray cut short to reveal (damp patch in corner). Tray and vertical dpc do not meet (damp patch in corner).

Check List		Walls 5
Element	*Symptom*	*Defect*
Openings (cont.)	Damp patch to reveal in cavity wall.	Defective or missing vertical dpc.
	Damp patch 6in-12in (150-230mm) above soffit of lintel.	Mortar droppings bridging tray.
	Sill or frame rotting from back.	Defective priming or omission of dpc in stock brickwork.
	Sill or frame rotting from inside building.	Probably due to condensation (kitchen or bathrooms).
	Sill or frames rotting from outside building.	Lack of maintenance.
	Damp stains on painted or papered walls at sill level, usually elongated, and extending full width of window board next to reveal (single glazing).	Condensation.
	Dirty spots on paper or painted plaster reveals especially next to metal windows fixed direct to structure.	Cold spot condensation.
	Ditto where timber windows are provided.	Cold spot condensation from suspected slate cavity closers.
	Ditto to heads of opening.	Cold spot condensation from concrete lintel usually in conjunction with steel supporting member to outer skin of cavity wall.
		Defective or missing damp course.

Check List	Floors and staircases 1	
Element	*Symptom*	*Defect*
Floors (timber)	Floor finish or boarding under and at the back of w.c.s, sinks and basins defective.	Leak in outgo of pan, in the trap or in the services.
	Floor and skirting to first floor bay window show signs of rot.	If the bay window is constructed wholly of timber there is the likelihood of wet rot in the timber framing.
	Floor to first floor bay dips outwards.	Ditto, or it may be settlement. (Check for cracking at junction with main wall of house.)
	First floor unstable under-foot. (Check for cracking of ceiling below.)	Excessive notching of joists for central heating installation.
	wedges omitted allowing springy floor	Ditto for rewire of electrical services.
		Herringbone strutting omitted.
		Joists seriously affected by infestation or rot.
	Boards creak underfoot.	Boarding not properly refixed after lifting.
	Ground floor unstable underfoot.	Defect in sleeper wall.
		Excessive notching of joists for services as described above.

excessive deflection due to notching of joists for services | |
| | Boarding stained in areas. | Rot in floor should be suspected. |
| | Perimeter of ground floor boarding is damp. | Rising damp with possibility of rot in joists and plate. |

Check List	Floors and staircases 2	
Element	*Symptom*	*Defect*
Floors (timber) (cont.)	Deep cracks or splits both along and across the grain of the timber.	Dry rot infection.
	White fluffy growth on timber.	Ditto.
	Long filaments over wood originating from soft, platelike fruiting body.	Ditto.
	Deep cracks along the grain of timber.	Cellar rot.
	Thin olive-green or brown fruiting body on surface of timber.	Ditto.
	Floors spongy and depressed under linoleum or other similar floor covering.	Attack of rot must be suspected.
Floors (solid)	Plastic tiles lifting next to skirtings.	Rising damp or bridging of damp course.
	Floor finishes rising or becoming generally detached (wood or plastic).	Rising damp.
	Quarry tiles loose.	Shrinkage in the subfloor has detached the tiles or these have been subjected to heavy impact.
Stairs (timber)	Staircase squeaks underfoot.	Check stair treads and risers are screwed and not nailed. Check blocking is present between treads and risers. Check wedges between string treads and risers are firmly glued.
	Treads fall away from wall to open well.	Defect in outer string.
	Small holes and attendant sawdust in open soffit of staircase.	Check for beetle infestation (see Roof).
	Bottom riser of stair has cracks or splits along the grain of wood.	Check for rot especially where the floor is solid underneath.

and likely remedial costs will be included in the report. Chemical degradation of the substrata, i.e., sulphates in mortar, will show on the surface by the:
○ Deposition of salts.
○ Breakdown of the surface of the finishing material.
○ Loose and flaking surfaces.
Cracking of the finishing material may be due to a number of reasons which may or may not be serious or structural:
○ Excessive shrinkage of the substrata structure can produce truly monumental cracking usually accompanied by loss of adhesion and large areas of loose plaster.
○ Cracks which produce deformation in the plane of the element, distortion of the structural fabric and are generally structural have been described previously on p. 55.
○ Shrinkage cracking due to differential drying shrinkage by materials in close promimity, where sufficient care has not been taken to bridge over the shrinkage lines to contain the movement. The classic example here is movement cracking at the juxtaposition of concrete and brick or block walling where the plaster is carried over the junction.
○ Cracking due to thermal movement, expansion or contraction, where slip joints and/or planes have not been incorporated in the structure and the consequential stresses have caused failure.
Most of these defects occur in new buildings. In older structures any cracking will have been made good over the years with general maintenance. New buildings are more prone to this form of defect due to excessively strong bricks and mortars used in their construction and general lack of care in their erection.

Walls

Walls in domestic properties are generally plastered, this finished in a number of ways to provide a decorative effect. Plaster is generally of two kinds:
○ Lime plaster in older properties applied in three coats either directly on to the surface of internal walls or on to timber laths and a batten secured to external walls where these are of solid construction (see p. 79).
○ A gypsum plaster in post-war properties applied in two coats directly on to all internal wall surfaces.

Check List	Internal finishes 1	
Element	*Symptom*	*Defect*
Walls and ceilings	Crack in solid plaster where the plaster is level on either side.	Shrinkage cracks.
	Crack where the plaster is detached but still level on either side.	Probably still shrinkage crack, but check for further signs of structural movement, if any.
	Crack in plaster where adjacent surfaces are distorted into different planes.	Cracks formed by distortion of the structure.
	Crack at junction of plastered walls and plaster lath and set to ceilings.	Shrinkage crack.
	Irregular surface of ceiling under lining paper in old property.	Plaster cracked or detached from lath – check for movement by gentle pressure from below. Also check wall surfaces.
	Wall surface soft and resilient under paper.	Check for polystyrene as damp barrier.
	Wall surface under paper gives continuous very high reading on moisture meter.	Check for foil lining as damp course.

Old lime plastered surfaces are usually covered with a network of fine hair cracks, usually concealed by lining paper. New plaster is often emulsioned directly on to the surface of the plaster which is smooth and satisfactory for such a finish. Occasionally new plaster 'crazy cracks' soon after application - usually due to excessive shrinkage or too rapid drying out of the finishing coat.

Damp penetration through external walls and rising damp internally can be kept back from the surface by the application of metal foil, a specially formulated plastic sheet covering, or a thin sheet of polystyrene. Care must be taken to identify these where they occur.

Permanent finishes can cause problems for the surveyor. They may include:

be infested, in most cases the floors will be affected also and the beetle will usually also be found in sapwood in the staircase. Fungal rot can also be found, usually spreading out from an infected lower floor through contact between the strings and the boarding.

Internal finishes

The primary object of a structural report is to advise on the structural condition of the property. Internal finishes are applied to the structure for two primary reasons:

○ As a cosmetic effect which may be changed repeatedly without affecting the basic strength or stability of the building, and

○ For hygienic reasons to seal the supporting structure from penetration by moisture or to enable the surfaces to be readily and easily cleaned.

Defects in applied finishes are due to a number of reasons, generally related to the care with which the occupants have used the building:

○ Abrasion or impact damaging the surface or breaking components such as wall and floor tiles. These defects are generally expensive to rectify – usually replacement units are difficult to obtain or match in the stripping out and total replacement is often necessary.

○ Lack of general cleaning or the failure to apply regular surface maintenance materials such as polish. The cost of refurbishing and polishing to renovate surfaces such as wood block flooring may be expensive.

○ The use of unsuitable surface cleaning methods resulting in loss of surface finish, or, in extreme cases, disintegration of the structure of the finish itself.

In addition, deterioration of the structure by chemical degradation, settlement cracking or thermal and moisture movement may well have been noticed and recorded under previous elements and the subsequent effect on surface finishes wil be apparent and their effect on the property value

Growth is most rapid in summer with a fruit body growing to about 300 mm, larger in severe outbreaks, coloured white/grey with a centre of rust red dust-like spores. The hyphae or filaments spread over timber and penetrate brickwork to spread the infection which shows as a linear 'blister' where it passes behind the surface of plaster. This fungal rot spreads with great rapidity, the mycelium growing as a white fluffy mass similar to cotton wool, and is characterised by a familiar 'mushroom' smell. Once established in a floor it will attack all timber and joinery with which it comes into contact.

Cellar rot (*Coniophora cerebella*) is wet rot (see photo) needing timber with a moisture content of at least 25 per cent and continuous wet conditions in which to grow. While cellar rot flourishes in wet conditions it does not have the ability to produce conditions for its own propagation and dies out on reaching dry structure. Removal of the cause of damp usually cures the trouble. Often found in boarded floors in wet situations such as kitchens and utility rooms where sheet materials such as vinyl cover the floor.

Serpulia lacrymans (dry rot) Crown copyright: reproduced by permission of the Building Research Establishment, Princes Risborough Laboratory

Coniophora cerebella (cellar rot)

Staircases

Domestic staircases are invariably constructed of timber and although design and layout may vary, the construction of all are similar.

If the soffit of the staircase is open the construction can be checked to see that:

○ The wedges are tight and well glued.

○ The splayed blocking is well glued and screwed.

○ The internal tongued joint between tread and riser is securely screwed from below to reduce the likelihood of squeaking.

If the soffit is plastered, jump up and down on the staircase treads to check that the above construction has been soundly carried out.

Staircases should be of reasonable width and have an easy going, not exceeding

2 x riser + tread = 600 mm

Balustrades should be checked for strength and stability. Newels should be housed into string and apron and not fixed only by dowels. Handrails should be firmly fixed to walls. Staircases and timber floors are prone to the same infestation by beetle as are roof structures. If the roof is found to

○ Traditional timber or a plywood panelling which may be affected by rot or beetle infestation. Free ventilation through the back from skirting to cornice is important to reduce the risk of moisture build-up between panelling and wall surface.

○ Mosaic or tesserae linings to bathrooms or cloakrooms which may well be impossible to repair or to replace missing pieces.

○ Vitrolite, which is generally bedded and pointed in plaster-of-paris and if cracked is very difficult to remove and to-day virtually impossible to replace.

○ Marble which, unless it has been kept well cleaned and polished, tends to become ingrained with dirt and difficult to clean.

○ Ceramic tiles which are of two kinds, only the modern 'cushion' tile being readily available, and colour matching, due to changing fashions, a problem.

All these special finishes should be carefully examined and defects and likely repair problems noted in the report.

Check List	Internal finishes 1	
Element	*Symptom*	*Defect*
Plaster walls	Surface covered with net of fine hair cracks.	Differential shrinkage between backing and setting coats.
	Surface soft under wallpaper.	Check whether wall is lined with polystyrene to repel damp. Check with moisture meter into backing.
	Area of plaster in old building bulges and gives under pressure.	Plaster laths are detached from grounds.
	Vertical cracks in plaster over door heads in partitions.	Shrinkage of frame and insufficient care in applying expanded metal lath as plaster ground.
	Cracks in plaster at heads of window frames.	Differential shrinkage between walls and lintels during drying out.

Check List	Internal finishes 2	
Element	*Symptom*	*Defect*
Plaster walls (cont.)	Vertical cracks in plaster following probable joints in brick or blockwork.	Differential shrinkage between blocks or bricks of differing composition at points of contact.
	Untidy cracking around heads of internal doors.	Cut work and pinning up to lintel carried out using small pieces of material, often of a composition different from mass, causing differential shrinkage.
	Vertical or horizontal crack in wall with the surfaces in the same plane.	Differential shrinkage probably due to stopping off the work for a period (vertical) or the block or brick wall finished against a frame member such as a concrete column.
	Ditto, where the surfaces on either side are in different planes.	Structural movement resulting in deformation of the surface plane. If the crack is wider at the top than at the bottom of a vertical crack, this indicates settlement.
	Vertical crack in corner of room.	Even width from top to bottom indicates shrinkage. Wider at top than at bottom indicates possible deflection in supporting member.
	Cracks around window boards and window frames.	Differential shrinkage between materials.
	Decorations or plaster disfigured with soft eruptions.	Deliquescent salts leaching out of wall structure on to face of plaster. In corners of new buildings often caused by urine.

Check List		Painting defects 3
Element	*Symptom*	*Defect*
Drying trouble	Description	Paint is tacky, soft or wet after an excessive length of time after application.
	Causes	Application in unsuitable weather. Application over bituminous or wax finish. Application over primer which has not hardened sufficiently. Use of unsuitable thinners.
Efflorescence	Description	A white crystalline or amorphous deposit forming on new brick, plaster or cement surfaces as water evaporates from them. It can also appear on old surfaces where moisture has penetrated.
	Causes	By soluble salts brought in solution from the substrate to the surface and deposited. When deposited beneath a paint film the surface is disrupted.
Flaking	Description	Paint lifting away or peeling back from a surface, usually from a split or joint in the film.
	Causes	Using incompatible primers or undercoats. Shrinkage or expansion of a substrate where the surface contains or can absorb water (wood sills). Application to powdery or chalky old paint where adhesion is unsatisfactory. Application to dirty, greasy surfaces providing poor intercoat adhesion.
Grinning	Description	Undercoat showing through the finishing coat.
	Causes	Poor workmanship. Using an undercoat of an unsuitable colour. Too wide a colour change with too few coats.

Check List		Painting defects 4
Element	*Symptom*	*Defect*
Loss of gloss	Description	Finish is flat and lifeless.
	Causes	Application to greasy or waxy surface.
		Application in unsuitable weather.
		Application to a porous undercoat or omission of the undercoat.
		Use of unsuitable thinners.
		Old age and beginning of chalking.
Misses	Description	Areas left uncoated.
	Causes	Poor workmanship exaggerated by the use of thick paint or application over greasy or moist surfaces.
Mould	Description	Usually a greyish or sooty spotting although some moulds are coloured or produce stains which colour the surface. Growth can be very rapid.
	Causes	A high moisture content or relative humidity in excess of 70per cent.
		A supply of organic material on which to feed.
Poor opacity	Description	Failure to obliterate the substrate.
	Causes	Overthinning of the paint.
		Failure to stir the paint thoroughly.
Running	Description	A sagging uneven wave to the surface finish.
	Causes	Over-application of paint.
		Application of further paint to wet edge which has started to set.
Saponification	Description	Oil paint turned into a soft sticky mass exuding drops or runs of a brown gummy liquid.
	Cause	Attack by a strong alkali on a paint film.

must be to report on the condition of the substrata (see p. 78). With joinery, the paintwork is not only decorative – it is primarily protective and its condition must be carefully examined and dealt with fully in the report. The adjacent schedule gives details of common blemishes and defects found in decorative work.

This section finishes with a brief description of fixed fittings such as those found in the kitchen, bedroom, fitted wardrobes, etc. Today, much of this is poor quality enamelled chipboard 'throw-away' stuff and often new owners strip this out to replace with similar. Where joinery is found this should be carefully noted and described in the report.

Check List		Painting defects 1
	Symptom	*Defect*
Bittiness	Description	Small hard excrescences on the surface of the paint.
	Cause	Dirt from atmosphere or from inadequately cleaned brushes or spray skin from paint which has been stirred in instead of being strained out.
Bleeding	Description	Discolouration or staining of a paint coating by the diffusion of coloured substances from beneath.
	Causes	Application over bituminous paints, tar, asphalt coatings, pitch impregnated or creosoted surfaces, red paints, etc., which have not been effectively sealed or removed.
Blistering	Description	Oval or raised areas of paintwork.
	Causes	Moisture or solvents trapped in the substrate below the paint film. Paint applied to wet surfaces. Trapped solvent when paint coats are applied in the direct heat of the sun.
Blooming	Description	A mist or haze on gloss finishes giving apparent loss of gloss.
	Causes	Moisture and contaminants in the atmosphere.

Check List		Painting defects 2
Element	*Symptom*	*Defect*
Brush marks	Description	Ribbed lines in the surface of the finish.
	Causes	Uneven or careless application. Continued brushing after the paint has set. Application when paint is too thick. Application with a dirty or clogged brush.
Chalking	Description	The formation of a fine powder on the paint film.
	Causes	A normal paint applied over insufficiently sealed porous surfaces. An inferior paint deficient in binder or vehicle. Finish mixed with undercoat.
Cissing	Description	Shrinkage or drawing away of new coating from areas of the work.
	Causes	Contamination of the atmosphere or surface from grease or oil. Silicones from polishes used on substrate. Exudation from an over-oily undercoat. Waterborne paints applied over oil-based paints (usually found in varnishes).
Crazing	Description	Irregular cracking of a surface coating penetrating one or more of the top coats.
	Causes	Old age. Application of hard drying paint over an undercoat which has not fully dried. Application of hard drying paints to soft bituminous surfaces.

Ceilings

The basic ceiling construction will have been established during the inspection carried out within the roof void. This will generally be as follows:

○ Older properties built before 1939; timber laths and plaster finish. Some plasterboard was used during this period, but only in very low quality work.

○ Properties built after 1945; plaster lath and skin coat

Check List		Internal finishes 3
Element	*Symptom*	*Defect*
Plaster ceilings	Crack around perimeter at wall and ceiling junction.	Differential shrinkage between materials.
	Long straight cracks across ceiling from wall to wall.	Deflection of supporting structure, possibly due to partition over or heavy loads in roof space.
	Plaster ceiling bellying below general level.	Timber laths off-key with supporting structure.
	U-shaped cracks in surface.	Plaster lath detached from supporting structure.
	Blister or small crater in finish surface.	Rusty nail or dirt in mix.
Joinery	Shrivelling and cracking of timber skirtings, material dry and crumbling to the touch.	Dry rot.
	External frames, etc., have splits and cracks with the run of the grain, material is crumbly and soft to the touch.	Wet rot.
	Glass in old steel windows cracked.	Rusty frames under paintwork.
	Pin holes in skirtings, door frames and linings with attendant sawdust.	Check for beetle infestation (see Roofs).
	Skirting is disfigured with cracking and is soft and crumbly to the touch.	Wet or dry rot (see Floors).

plaster. In some properties plasterboard in large sheets will be found, the joints between boards showing as shrinkage cracks, a problem which is generally absent using the smaller sized laths.

Older properties are often provided with cornice and centre rose embellishments which are often coarse and heavy in execution. The weight of plaster and deterioration of the brads securing the laths to the joists often cause such features to become detached. Many such ceilings are papered over – often this is applied to hide cracks which usually indicate loose plaster. War-time bombing was often a cause of such defects.

Joinery and wood trim

The three main matters to be considered in the inspection of joinery and trim are:
○ The standards of material used and workmanship employed.
○ Freedom from organic rots and beetle infestation.
○ The standard of decoration, quality of materials used and workmanship employed.

Good material will provide joinery which is straight and true, free from shrinkage cracks, large knots and the need to employ large amounts of filling to level up the surface for decoration. However, good material will deteriorate quickly under conditions of damp or excessive heat which will dry out the timber causing excessive shrinkage. These points should be borne in mind when making an assessment of material quality.

The standard of workmanship employed will be reflected in the finished article. Mitres to architraves should be accurately and closely cut. Skirtings should be scribed to the floor and one to another in internal angles. External angles should be neatly close mitred. Frames and linings should be square, upright and the doors hung with even gap all round.

All items cut and fitted together should be a tight close fit, plumb and square.

With decorations, these are, so far as colour and texture are concerned, very much a personal matter. As most properties are re-decorated on re-occupation, apart from special permanent finishes mentioned before, the main consideration

Check List		Painting defects 5
Element	*Symptom*	*Defect*
Sheeriness	Description	Uneven gloss or more especially glossy patches and streaks on flat or eggshell finishes.
	Causes	Uneven application giving different paint thicknesses. Application over partially set paint resulting in a thick edge.
Shrivelling	Description	Wrinkling on parts of paint surfaces too heavily coated.
	Causes	Unevenly applied paints where a skin forms on the thicker areas and prevents the film drying evenly, especially in hot sun and drying wind.

Drainage

Once installed and then forgotten – out of sight and out of mind. Regular inspection, flushing through and clearance of gullies are important to keep underground drains in good working order, a condition rarely found.

Property drainage can be separated into two distinct parts:

○ Pipework with its attendant collection gullies, collection and interception chambers and associated fittings constructed below the surface of the ground, and

○ Collection pipework, soil and ventilation stacks situated either in ducts within the building structure or exposed on the external face of the building.

Testing is carried out to ensure that not only are the various components in proper air or watertight condition, but that they are able to transport and dispose of effluent and waste speedily and without loss.

The location, opening up of covers to manholes and the location of drain runs will have been carried out immediately the surveyor and builder arrive on site (see p. 15). At this point a careful sketch plan of the drainage system will be prepared and annotated as shown on the sketch. This will provide a clear visual reference to the notes on the check list prepared during the testing of the installation.

The outfall of foul drainage can be to either:

○ The local authority sewer in the road.

○ A common drain serving a number of properties in close proximity to one another and passing through the various plots to eventually discharge in the local authority sewer.

○ To a common drain serving a number of properties and discharging into a private sewage disposal plant.

○ Direct to a cesspool or septic tank installation located within the site boundaries.

A full description of the method of disposal should appear in the report and any irregularities under the Public Health Acts drawn to the attention of the prospective purchaser.

Instructions for the preparation of drainage sketch plan:

○ Each manhole should be numbered, commencing from the head of the system.

○ Each gully should be shown, given a reference letter and a note made of the fittings discharging into it.

○ Drain runs connected to ground floor w.c. pans, s + vp's and vent shafts should be so noted.

○ Each s + vp, vent shaft or one-pipe stack should be provided with a reference letter.

○ The positions of interceptor traps, fresh air inlets and rodding eyes where found should be indicated on the drawing.

○ Cesspools and septic tanks should be indicated together with positions of discharge manholes and likely position of subsoil drainage runs.

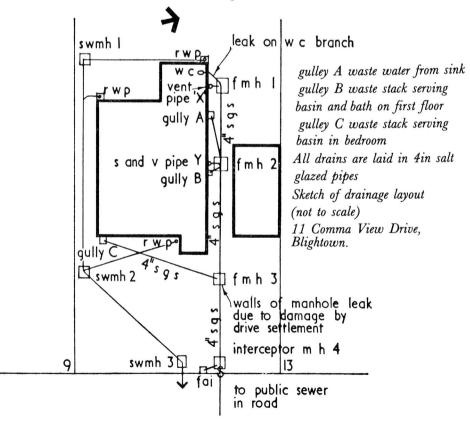

gulley A waste water from sink
gulley B waste stack serving basin and bath on first floor
gulley C waste stack serving basin in bedroom
All drains are laid in 4in salt glazed pipes
Sketch of drainage layout (not to scale)
11 Comma View Drive, Blightown.

○ The diameters of drains should be indicated on runs and the positions of any change in bore or material used carefully noted.

The outfall of stormwater can be to either:

○ A combined drainage system incorporating foul and stormwater within the same drain runs.

○ A separate stormwater drainage system with its own manholes and connection to a local authority stormwater sewer or water authority controlled water course.

○ By discharge directly into pits known as soakaways.

Generally storm water discharge into soakaways is by direct connection of the rainwater pipe into the socket of the drain at ground level. Stormwater drainage systems required a trapped gully to be provided to receive the discharge from the rwp.

The Public Health Act requirements for domestic drainage incorporated into the standards required for building require access to be provided at certain points to enable drain runs to be properly inspected and maintained in working conditions. Blockage of drains occurs either:

○ Through the introduction of solid matter too heavy for the natural velocity of the water in the system to move to the discharge point, and backing up by other solids until the pipe is blocked.

○ Settlement in the pipe runs causing a low point in the system which can only clear liquids by syphoning, solids being left behind to cause a blockage.

○ Crushing of the pipe by a heavy load such as vehicle wheel loads causing a blockage from debris and the backing up of foul solids.

Access points for rodding and clearing of blockages are generally necessary at:

○ Changes of direction in the drain run.

○ Change of inclination of the drain run.

○ At the junction of two drains carrying solid foul matter in suspension.

○ At distances not exceeding 18 metres apart.

Manholes are constructed in a number of different ways, incorporating different materials:

○ One brick thick walls finished fair face.

○ Half brick thick walls rendered internally to make them waterproof.

○ Precast concrete, either monolithic or in a number of segments.
○ uPVC to suit proprietary plastic drainage systems.

All should be sound and watertight and provided with an air-tight cover. If of cast iron or steel, such covers should be provided with proper lifting lugs and properly set in grease into their frames.

All vent shafts, one-pipe stacks (where visible), soil and vent shafts and waste stacks, should be inspected and their description included in the report indicating material composition, diameter, effectiveness under test and identified on the sketch plan.

Waste heads and externally exposed waste pipes from sanitary fittings and sinks are potentially susceptible to damage from frost.

The location of cesspools and septic tanks should be noted and some indication of their likely capacity given. Check that each is provided with:

○ An interceptor manhole and fresh air vent to isolate the installation from the house drainage system.
○ Proper and well-sealed covers; defective covers are both a health and a safety hazard.
○ Where land drainage outfall is provided, this should spread out from a manhole on the outgo of the system and an inspection of this manhole will show whether the system is operating satisfactorily and whether the land drainage system is working properly.

Testing drains

Before a drainage system can be considered fit for use it is a requirement of the Public Health Acts that it be watertight. During the operative life of the system various factors can produce defects which may cause the drains to leak. Consequently during an inspection for a Structural Survey Report it is necessary to carry out tests to check the efficiency of the system. Three types of test are in current use:

○ The smoke test which is most suitable for testing pipes and shafts above ground after sealing off the sections by means of the water filled trap to the connected fittings and an expanding plug set into the manhole branch.
○ The hydraulic test which is general for new drain runs, but when applied to old drains can exert pressure on pipes

and joints which, while satisfactory in normal use, would fail under pressures exerted by the head of water used.

○ The pneumatic test which is best used for installations of some age, where a uniform pressure is applied to all parts of the pipework, and leakage is indicated either by a fall in pressure or the inability to raise any pressure at all.

The smoke test is carried out by first sealing the top of the stack with a drain plug, introducing smoke into the respective branch drain connecting the stack to the manhole and then sealing this with a drain plug. Smoke rockets can be used to produce the smoke, but because the smoke is not produced under pressure it is often difficult to force smoke to the top of the shaft. Consequently the use of a smoke machine is advisable. Smoke produced from ignited bituminous roofing felt or a similar material is put under pressure from a bellows and transferred through a flexible pipe to the inlet on the drain plug. The build up of pressure will force the smoke up the drain and shaft and visual inspection will indicate any defective joints or cracks in the shaft or waste pipes to fittings.

The usual points of weakness are:

○ The joint between the shaft and the socket of the drain, and
○ The joint between the outgo of the pan and the soil branch.

Settlement can cause the first to fail and shrinkage in the timber suspended floor can cause the pan joint to fail. The use of plastic close fit connectors tends to remove this problem.

Defects found in the soil and vent shafts should be noted in detail and the precise location of defects should be noted in the report.

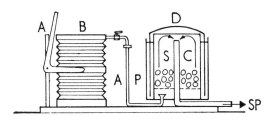

SC smoke chamber   SP smoke pipe
D dome set in water jacket   B double bellows
AP air pipe   A level
Diagram showing operation of smoke machine (not to scale).

Check List		Drainage 1
Element	*Symptom*	*Defect*
Soil and vent pipe Vent shaft One-pipe stacks	Shaft and drain connection to manhole do not hold to test (smoke test).	Drain fractured under ground (check for smoke emission at junction of drain and manhole wall or where pipe issues from ground). Defective joint between drain and shaft (smoke emission at joint). Fracture or bad joint in shaft (smoke emission from defect). Defective joint between w.c. pan and shaft branch (smoke in building). Bad joint on one-pipe stack (smoke emission from defect). Drain connecting one-pipe shaft to manhole fractured where it passes through foundations due to pressure or settlement (smoke under suspended ground floor, or in roof space through open top of shaft casing, or emission from ground next to wall of building).
Gulleys	Fitting and drain do not hold up to test (hydraulic or pneumatic).	Drain fractured under ground. Joint between gully and drain defective. Gully cracked.

The hydraulic test should be restricted to drainage systems not more than 10 - 15 years old and then only after careful inspection of the manholes to ensure that the standard of workmanship employed in the drainage works is sufficient to withstand the pressures to be applied.

The system should be tested in sections, commencing at the top manhole. Before commencing the next section, insert a plug in the inlet pipe to the next manhole and introduce water gradually from the upper section to enable air in the pipework to be slowly released. Before checking levels, bleed the section through the plug to ensure that all air has been expelled. Points to remember in hydraulic testing are:

○ W.C. branches should be tested by filling the pan up to the underside of the rim to simulate pressures caused by flushing.

○ Water levels in manholes should be marked, the depth filled should be at least 600 mm.

○ Allowance must be made for absorption in rendered manhole walls – the absorption in fair brick manholes is minimal.

○ Always check that drain plugs are sound fitted and not leaking.

○ A leak in a defective drain run can be located with some accuracy by floating a bag plug down the drain, inflating it at intervals and refilling the drain with water.

The pneumatic test used on old drainage systems is quick and positive. Each end of the drain is plugged, one end sealed and the other attached to a smoke machine. Operation of the bellows raises the pressure under the dome which rises in the water:

○ If the level of the dome remains constant there is no leakage of air in the drain which is consequently sound.

○ If the dome subsides the length of drain is defective.

When using this method for main runs it is advisable to check branches to wcs and gullies by a hydraulic test. The water so used can be collected in successive manholes to test these for leakage.

If the drains are found to be in order, it is only necessary to include in the report:

○ A brief description of their construction.

○ The type of test carried out on each section.

○ A statement that at the date of the inspection the drains were satisfactory.

Any defects found should be briefly described in such a manner as to be easily located by reference to the drainage sketch plan.

Check List	Drainage 2	
Element	*Symptom*	*Defect*
Manholes	Manholes filled to top of flaunching and water disperses (hydraulic test).	Check drain plug in outgo is not leaking. Check joint between inlet and outgo pipes and rendering for leaks. Check joints between channel and flaunching for leaks. Check channel for defect in jointing or cracks.
	Channels dirty with soil or silt.	Insufficient fall to clear soil. If the drain is found to leak badly there may be an ingress of fine material from the surrounding area.
Drain runs	Drain between manhole does not hold up to test (pneumatic or hydraulic).	Check drain plugs are not leaking. Slow loss of water or pressure probably due to defective joint. Heavy loss of pressure or water probably due to fracture or crushing of the pipe especially under drives.
Ground floor wc	Drain connection between pan and manhole does not hold to test (smoke test).	Bad joint between pan and drain (smoke in building). Drain connecting pan and manhole fractured where it passes through foundation wall due to pressure or settlement (smoke under floor or emission from ground next to external face of wall).

Services

The services installed within a domestic property account for a large percentage of its initial cost and as, in general, their life expectancy is about 30 - 50 per cent of that of the structure, and their replacement costs high, their condition and operating efficiency is an important matter for the house owner. Services can be divided into:

○ Wet services comprising the supply and distribution of drinking, cold and hot water.
○ Heating installation.
○ Gas services.
○ Electrical services.

Each of these requires to be inspected by a competent specialist whose individual reports will be added to the structural report prepared by the surveyor.

Supply service and rising main

The inspection commences at the point of supply and checks should be made in the sequence in which the water circulates. With residential properties the water authorities main is usually situated under the road or footway, and at the point of entry to the site will be found a stop tap. This should be examined and the following points checked:

○ The depth of the service pipe at this point – not less than 750 mm or frost damage may occur.
○ Any sign of leakage on the consumer's side of the stop tap.
○ The material used for the service pipe (lead or galvanised iron indicate an old installation).

The householder's stop tap may be found in one of several

places, generally within the property and usually situated just above the ground floor level. The procedure for checking the stop tap is:

○ If the house is occupied and the stop tap open, close the tap and check its efficiency by opening the cold tap at the kitchen sink. No water will flow if the stop tap functions correctly.

○ If the house is unoccupied and the stop tap closed, open it and the sound of flowing water will confirm its efficient function.

Most water authorities require a drain cock to be fitted next to the stop tap to drain the rising main. To check that this is working properly, place a bucket under the drain cock, close the stop tap and open the cock. If this works correctly water should flow into the bucket. After closing the cock check that no water flows from the outlet or from around the spindle of the stop tap indicating faulty packing.

The age and satisfactory functioning of the rising main may be found by visual inspection:

○ Old installations are composed of lead or galvanised iron pipe situated on the inner face of the external wall. Signs of repair indicate past frost damage, excessive water pressure or electrolytic damage, all faults commonly found in lead piping.

○ Modern installations are composed of copper, polythene or pvc piping and the rising main is situated on an internal wall at least 450 mm from the external.

Check that there are no blockages in the main and that flow is adequate by depressing the cistern ball valve. The pressure should be adequate and discharge continuous and full bore. Check that the rising main is continuously located where there is little likelihood of frost damage occurring and that the pipe is fully lagged throughout its length.

Cold water distribution system

Cold water storage cisterns have been dealt with previously in Chapter 8. These cisterns must be fitted with an overflow pipe at least one size larger than the supply service to safeguard against a faulty ball valve.

The distribution pipe should be traced and carefully examined for leaks. An isolating gate valve should be fitted close to the outlet from the cistern, and in good quality work, one will be installed next to each appliance such as the w.c. cistern. Each gate valve should be checked to confirm that it operates correctly and that there are no leaks around the spindle or joints with the feed pipe.

The pipework may be composed of materials as previously described for the rising main and the same comments apply. The pipe runs should be inspected for:

○ Physical defects to the outside of the pipe caused by a blow or pressure - such defects or damage can lead to future leaks.

○ Corrosion of copper pipes due to dezincification or electrolytic action - pin holes in the pipe which leak.

○ Extensions carried out to the installation to serve extra fittings without increasing the bore of the original pipework. The supply to the fittings will be low, sluggish or negligible in the worst cases.

Hot water distribution systems

A hot water system incorporating a boiler as the heat source consists of:

○ The cold feed to the heating appliance.

○ The hot water cylinder.

○ The primary circulating pipes.

○ The expansion pipe.

○ The hot supply to the sanitary fittings.

The volume of hot water available to a property is controlled by:

○ The output rating of the heating appliance which is dealt with later in this section, and

○ The capacity of the hot water cylinder.

This capacity is generally laid down in the local water authority by-laws, but as a general rule the following applies:

○ 2 br house - 3 persons - 112 litres capacity

○ 3/4 br house - 4/5 persons - 135 litres capacity

○ 5 br house - 6/7 persons - 157 litres capacity.

Cylinders are now generally made from copper sheet, domed top and bottom and situated in the linen cupboard. They should be:

○ Raised off the floor on timber blocks to prevent condensation forming on the underside.

○ Free from corrosion around outlets and immersion heater boss.

○ Free from any dents or abrasions.

Many new cylinders are supplied with an integral lagging making it impossible to check for corrosion. Generally the life of a cylinder does not exceed 25 years and this can be used as a guide to its likely condition. Any galvanised cylinders or hot water tanks should be recommended for replacement.

The material used for hot water systems are galvanised iron and copper and the same comments apply. The running cost of a hot water system depends on a number of factors which should be taken into account when assessing its efficiency:

○ All hot pipework and cylinder surfaces should be properly lagged.

○ The hot water cylinder should be situated relatively close to the heating appliance.

○ The lengths of hot supply pipe runs should not exceed 4 - 5 metres.

○ No 'dead legs' over 4 - 5 metres.

○ The provision of a gate valve to isolate each section of the installation.

The furring-up of pipes and appliances is the most common problem found in hot water installations. This is common in hard water areas where calcium carbonate in solution heated above 82°C forms a deposit of chalk on the inner walls of pipes, cylinder and heating appliance. Two methods of assessing the degree of deposition in a very rough and ready way are:

○ To tap alternately adjoining cold and hot feed pipes - a dull sound will indicate a blocked or partly blocked pipe.

○ Inspection of the outlet of hot water taps for encrustation and checking the difference of flow between hot and cold taps.

If either test indicates positive furring-up the prospective purchaser should be recommended to have the system broken into as near as possible to the heating source, by disconnecting the flow pipe from the boiler unions after draining the system. The use of a proprietary brand solvent diluted in the cold water storage tank can relieve the problem.

Check List	Services 1	
Element	*Symptom*	*Defect*
Stopcocks, etc.	Leakage around spindle. Metallic grating on operation.	Faulty packing due to age. Worn or disintegrated washer.
Draincock	No discharge when valve is opened.	Washer stuck to valve seating due to excess pressure or age.
	Water stain and encrustation around outlet.	Faulty washer.
Rising main	Excessive number of joints (lead pipe).	Main vulnerable to frost. Excessive pressure in old pipe. Soft water affecting pipe walls.
	Water pressure sluggish.	Blockage of pipe, possibly due to jointing material. Indentation of pipe wall.
	Noisy when water is running.	Loose fittings, broken saddles, corroded screws and fixings loose from walls.
Cold water services	Excessive number of joints.	Pipework vulnerable to frost.
	Signs of corrosion to external walls of pipes.	Copper to zinc in direct contact producing electrolytic action. Dezincification (check with water supply company).
	Supply is sluggish or nil with all taps open.	Pipe sizes are inadequate. Obstruction in bore. Insufficient head of water.
Hot water services cylinder	Corrosion to access plate of galvanised cylinder. Rust spots on surface.	Faulty gasket. Internal corrosion. General internal corrosion.

Check List	Services 2	
Element	*Symptom*	*Defect*
Pipework	Delay in discharge of hot water after tap opened.	Pipe runs too long. Pipes not lagged. Excessive dead legs.
	Sluggish discharge with encrustation around tap outlets.	Furred pipes.
	Water discharges around top of tap spindle.	Faulty packing or worn spindle.
	Tap continues to run after being turned off.	Faulty washer or worn valve seating.

Heating installation and applicances

Space heating is provided by one or a combination of the following systems:
○ Radiation.
○ Conduction.
○ Convection.
Appliances used in heating installations are generally complex and their variety are legion. They can be divided into:
○ Unit heaters, e.g., open fires or closed stoves, electric storage heaters, gas convectors, etc.
○ Central heating, using a variety of heat emitters.
Unit heaters should be itemised and their individual details and locations noted.
Open fireplaces should be checked for:
○ Open grate, underfloor draught, all-night burner.
○ Cracking in the plaster over the surround indicating absence of efficient throat lintel.
○ Dislodged tiles, etc., on the surround.
○ Fireclay back for cracking or disintegration.
○ Smoke stains indicating smoky flue.
Convection units installed as a replacement to an open fire should be checked for:
○ Distortion of the door allowing uncontrolled air to enter the fire compartment.
○ Cracks in or failure of the outer casing due to overheating.
○ Defects in sealing against air penetration.

Gas or electric fires should be checked to ensure that:
○ Appliance operates correctly at the various settings.
○ General condition is good.
○ Gas fire burners and ancillaries are in clean, sound order and undamaged.
○ Electric fires are connected with sound heavy quality heat-resisting cable and that connections are properly made.
Electric storage heaters should be in a similar condition to electric fires, remembering that in most cases they provide background heating only where installed in living areas.
Central heating incorporates a wide variety of different forms of space heating fired or powered by solid fuel, gas, oil or electricity. An inspection should be made by a specialist engineer who will generally check:
○ The primary circuit water is not discoloured by rust caused by corrosion within the radiators.
○ Lock-shield and control valves for leaks.
○ The accelerator operates correctly.
○ Small bore pipework, where installed, is undamaged and the flow unrestricted.
○ The installation is securely fixed to the structure.
○ Inspect the boiler for corrosion, damage or distortion, leaks, etc., and, in respect of gas or oil-fired boilers, the inspecting firm's record of servicing, replacements and repairs.
○ The installation and functioning of the mixer valve and automatic controls adjusting the flow temperature of the installation.
○ The time switch operates correctly.
In addition, where warm air systems are installed the following checks should be made:
○ All fans are operating correctly.
○ Fan bearings for wear.
○ All air intakes are clean and offer a free air flow.
The life expectation of boilers, apart from intermediate burner replacement, is about 15 -20 years and while the exact period of possible future working life is difficult to estimate, all boilers of obsolete patterns should be deemed ready for replacement in the near future.
The output of solid fuel, gas and oil-fired boilers is generally recorded on the appliance. For domestic hot water for a family of 4 - 6 persons a back boiler rated at 5 kw will serve

Home type	Aspect	Boiler Rating Space heating only	Space and domestic hot water
3 br semi-detached	Normal	12 kW	16 kW
3 br detached	Exposed	15 kW	20 kW
4 br detached	Normal	17 kW	20 kW

under normal conditions. For combined water and space heating the adjacent guide may be consulted.

Immersion heaters are installed as either:

○ A primary source of hot water supply, or

○ As a secondary source for summer use.

The simple mechanism of an electric immersion heater either does or does not work. Of 3 kW normal rating, its operation can be judged by checking the revolution of the meter disc when the heater switch is in the ON and OFF positions.

Gas circulators are often installed new or to convert an existing hot water installation. Usually installed adjacent to the hot water cylinder, the circulation must be able to discharge products of combustion to open air. This equipment is generally serviced by the local gas board and their service record should be checked.

Instantaneous water heaters are either gas or electric powered and can be divided into two types:

○ Those suitable for providing a supply of hot water to a single draw-off point and referred to as single-point heaters.

○ Those suitable for providing a supply of hot water to not more than three draw-off points and referred to as multi-point heaters.

Electric water heaters either work or they don't. Again, gas heaters are generally serviced by the local gas board whose service record should be checked. If a gas board official is unavailable:

○ Remove outer casing.

○ Check pilot light flame height of 25 mm.

○ Check mechanism and burners clean and free from grease.

○ Ensure that main burners ignite without undue delay immediately hot water tap is turned on.

Gas instantaneous water heaters of the single-point type do

not need a flue. Multi-point gas water heaters rated 2kW and over do, and most are now connected to a balanced flue discharging to the open air. These flues must be free from all obstructions.

Flues and chimneys

Domestic properties built before 1965 will have brick flues rendered internally with cement and sand. Where such flues are connected to or have previously been connected to slow-burning solid fuel appliances there is the risk that the lining and mortar joints of the flue structure are suffering from sulphate attack. This problem has been described before in Chapter 8.

Domestic properties constructed after 1965 will have flues lined with approved clay flue liners suitable for Class I appliances (i.e., those fired by solid fuel or oil). Gas appliances generally have a very much lower flue temperature which, coupled with water vapour and chemicals present in exuded flue gases, can cause serious sulphate problems to traditional rendered flues. They need to be provided with a specialist flexible flue liner formulated and fabricated specially for such boilers and heating sources.

The constitution of the various flues and the appliances connected to them should be described in the report and any recommendations for upgrading should be made.

Gas installation

While various gas appliances, their operation and condition, have been described in the sections dealing with water heating, the installation carcassing must be considered if a full picture of this part of the services installation is to be obtained.

Most properties in urban areas constructed over the past 100 years will have had gas installed. Where the pipework can be inspected its condition should be assessed with a view to renewal if iron pipework is corroded. In many cases this replacement will have been carried out by the local gas board who will advise on this matter. Where pipework is buried in the structure and visual inspection is impossible the gas board should be requested to test the installation and report on its condition. The test will involve:

Check List	Services 2	
Element	*Symptom*	*Defect*
Immersion heater	No variation in meter dial speed when heater switched on.	Faulty supply connection. Defective thermostat. Burnt-out element.
	Encrustation around boss.	Leak due to faulty joint.
Instantaneous water heater (gas)	Poor discharge. Lack of temperature.	Low mains pressure. Furred waterways. Dirty gas jets. Insufficient gas supply. Dirt, grease or dust on water-ways.
	Main gas jet fails to ignite.	Pilot light failure. Pilot light too small to 'flash' main burner.
	Heater smells when lighted.	Faulty flue. Dirty inlet of balanced flue. Accumulated grease on flueless heater.
Gas installation	Old installation.	Underground pipework likely to have corroded – see gas board.
Fuel storage oil	General corrosion on tank surfaces.	Lack of maintenance.

○ Isolating the main valve and meter.
○ Filling the pipework with air to a pressure of 350 mm wg.
○ Checking any drop in pressure by means of a manometer attached to any part of the installation.

Inefficient gas-burning appliances can be checked and tested as follows:

○ Note the appliance rating as shown on the manufacturer's name plate.
○ Ignite the burner(s) for a predetermined period (3 minutes will usually suffice).
○ Check number of cubic feet of gas consumed during this period by reference to the meter test tried, as described above.

The total consumption should be three times the consump-

tion/minute given by the manufacturer of the appliance.
All gas taps should be checked for easy, firm action and a
schedule of any defects and a copy of the report on the condition of the carcassing should be included in the survey.

Electrical installation

The electrical installation of a property is tested for the following reasons:
○ To ensure that it is safe to operate under normal usage,
  and
○ To enable the likely performance and probable life span
  of the installation to be drawn to the attention of the purchaser.
It is an advantage to be able to identify and date with some
accuracy the various types of electrical installation, and their
characteristics are given in the adjoining schedule. Many
installations that pre-date PVC are still in service and will
now need replacement.
The inspection is carried out following a similar procedure
to that for water services, starting at the intake position as
follows:
○ Note the position of the main cable intake, either
  underground or overhead supply.
○ Check that the intake is either of the armoured variety
  (diameter about 25mm) or cased in trunking from point
  of entry to position of boards cut-out.
○ Check that the loop in cables from cut-out to meter to
  control gear are in good condition.
○ Check that the control gear is of a modern consumer pattern or recommend replacement.
○ Check arrangement of circuits in consumer unit, usually
  as follows:
  30 amp – Cooker
  30 amp – Ring main circuit no. 1
  30 amp – Ring main circuit no. 2
  15 amp – Immersion heater
   5 amp – Lighting circuit no. 1
   5 amp – Lighting circuit no. 2
Where an eight-way unit is installed these will be arranged as:
   5 amp – bell transformer
  15 amp – spare way.

Locate each circuit by isolating each in turn with lamps and equipment switched ON.

○ Inspect each circuit to determine type of cable used. This can be done in the roof space, at switch and socket outlet positions, etc.

○ Check cables in roof space are properly fixed with clips at 225 - 300 mm centres and no lengths are under tension.

○ Check exposed conduit ends are properly bushed or smoothed off to avoid abrasion.

Two tests are carried out on the installation to determine its performance:

○ Circuits are tested at the mains position by first isolating the installation from the mains supply and then connecting a megohmeter to circuit terminals.

○ Each circuit is tested from:
   - phase to earth
   - neutral to earth
   - phase to neutral.

The tests are carried out to ensure that the insulation resistance has not broken down and will also indicate the presence of moisture and age of cables. Readings in sound insulations should not fall below 1 megohm. Readings below this level indicate an unsatisfactory installation. In new installations in empty buildings cold or damp conditions can give a false low reading.

○ The earthing of the circuits is tested by means of an earth-loop tester plugged into socket outlets with the main switch in the ON position. Any reading recorded above 1 ohm indicates a faulty earthing circuit.

Certain features of the installation should be looked for as they indicate an unsatisfactory installation:

○ Cables to pendant drops exposed to the air deteriorate quickly and their insulation becomes quickly defective.

○ Switch plates, socket outlets, etc., should be properly fixed and in sound condition.

○ Long length of flexible cable to equipment is unsatisfactory and heat-resisting cable should be used for all heat-producing appliances.

○ All fixed electrical equipment should be cabled on a separate circuit controlled by a switched fused spur outlet.

○ Socket outlets should be square 3 pin 13 amp standard pattern.

○ Bell transformers should be isolated by a separate 5 amp insulated isolating switch.

○ Lighting switches in bathrooms should be cord pull patterns and any fixed electrical equipment should be controlled by an isolating switch situated outside the bathroom. Proper shaver sockets should be provided.

The main earthing device for the installation should not be connected to the water main due to the increased use of alkathene for water mains. The earth should be:

○ Either bonded on to the main supply cut-out by means of a metal clip and green 7.044 or 6.00 mm cable, or an earth leakage circuit breaker should be incorporated.

The report on the electrical installation should include a schedule of lighting points, socket outlets and other items to complete the installation, together with an estimate of the cost of renewing or rectifying defects in the installation.

Electrical Systems – details and characteristics

Approx. date	Name and characteristics
1900 - 1920	'Capping and Casing' System Cable – vulcanised India-rubber with cotton braid Installation – surface with wooden trough cover Switches – brass cover tumbler on wooden base Ceiling roses – china pattern Sockets – 2 pin flush with brass cover plate Fuseboards – wooden box with glass front and china fuse holders
1910 - 1939	'Lead' System Cable – lead sheathed Installation – lead cable on surface with connector boxes Switches – surface tumbler with brass cover plates Remainder of fittings as 'Capping and Casing'
1925 - 1935	'Mackanite' System Cable – tough rubber insulated Installation – surface Fittings as 'Capping and Casing'

Approx. date	Name and characteristics
1928 - 1939	'Pin Grips' System Cable – vulcanised India-rubber with cotton braid Installation – metal conduit with unions, generally on surface Switches – surface tumbler on wood blocks with brass or brown plastic covers Ceiling roses – china Socket outlets – 2 pin Switch gear – cast iron with lighting circuits controlled by switch fuse with china base and brown plastic cover.
1935 - 1960	'Lug Grip' System Cable – vulcanised India-rubber with cotton braid Installation – metal conduit similar to 'Pin Grip'.
1925 - 1960	'Cabtyre' System Cable – tough rubber sheathed Installation – in voids in floors and walls, switch traps in metal conduit Switches – flush or surface, tumbler, wood blocks or boxes Ceiling roses – plastic Socket outlets – surface or flush, 2 or 3 round pin Switchgear – single or double pole.
1950 -	'PVC' System Cable – pvc insulated (grey or white) Installation – as 'Cabtyre' – since 1967 all outlets, switches, etc., will have separate earthed cable Switches – plastic flush or surface Socket outlets – general purpose 3 pin 13 amp with square pins Switch gear – single pole in a single consumer unit box with either cartridge fuses or circuit breaker isolators

Layout for the report on the electrical installations	
Intake and distribution	description
	arrangement of circuits
Circuit wiring	Description
(*continuity tests*)	Insulation *resistance*
	polarity
	earth
Ring circuits	ditto
Immersion heater	ditto
Lighting circuits	Insulation and polarity tests
Age of installation	
Defects if any (including work necessary to bring installation up to requirements of the latest IEE Regulations)	
Potential hazards	
Approximate estimate of cost of remedial works	
Schedule of points	

Check List	Services 3	
Element	*Symptom*	*Defect*
Heating open fires	Tiled surround sounds hollow.	Tiles free from backing.
	Crack over fire opening.	Fire overheats.
		Ineffective throat lintel.
	Fireclay backing cracked.	Movement due to overheating.
		Poor quality fireclay.
		Bad jointing.
Back boilers	Rust stain on face.	Leak to joint of access plate.
		Cracked boiler casing.
		Corrosion of retaining bolts.

Check List		Services 3
Element	*Symptom*	*Defect*
Boilers	Signs of leakage between boiler sections.	Faulty joints.
		Cracked section.
	Water leaks from safety valve.	Faulty valve seating.
		Weak main spring.
		Defective joint.
	Uncontrolled temperature in solid fuel boiler.	Badly fitting access door.
		Machined faces broken or corroded.
		Air flap not seating correctly.
		Defective boiler flue outlet.
		Incorrect setting of primary air inlet.
Central heating	Discoloured water from radiator vents.	Mixing of primary and secondary circuits forming corrosion.
	Water leaking from top of glandless radiator valves.	Faulty 'O' rings.
		Defective valve seatings (where applicable).
	Noisy accelerator.	Worn motor bearings.
	Undue play on fan blades of heater units.	Worn bearings.
Flues and chimneys	Black 'fungus' on face of chimney breast.	Ineffective dpc.
		Defective flashing.
		Lack of flue lining allowing condensation to penetrate structure.

External works

Boundaries to all properties should be clearly defined either:
○ By physical barriers, or
○ By clear and unambiguous description in the deeds of the property.
In addition all features forming the physical barriers should be in good condition: fences and walls are expensive items to repair or replace, apart from any legal problems which might arise if they were subsequently found to be unsound or dangerous.
The term boundary has no special meaning in law, being used to describe an imaginary line delineating the limit of a freehold or leasehold property. A boundary may, in fact, be indicated by a physical feature, e.g., a wall, a hedge or a ditch. Boundaries are therefore a matter of fact and of evidence, but common law does not impose any obligation on a landowner to erect and maintain a fence - it is, however, a convenient practice to do so, not only to mark the boundary but also to keep out intruders.
Boundaries can be divided into two kinds:
○ Natural boundaries such as rivers or streams, and
○ Man-made boundaries which include fences and rights of way.
Natural boundaries such as rivers or streams usually have the line of demarcation coinciding with the centre of the water course. With artifical watercourses the bed of the stream is usually conveyed to one or other of the adjoining owners, or to a third party and ownership will be a matter of evidence. With highways and rights of way, in the absence of evidence to the contrary, the subsoil belongs to the owners of the

adjoining properties.

Where a property adjoins a railway line, there is a statutory obligation for British Rail to fence, but this liability lapses when the line is removed.

Where two properties are divided by a hedge and an artificial ditch, or a ditch and a bank, the presumption is that the boundary is along the edge of the ditch furthest from the hedge or bank.

It should be borne in mind that plans annexed to conveyances show the position at ground level whereas it may well be that foundations and eaves project beyond the defined boundary line. This state of affairs does not exclude these features from the conveyed premises.

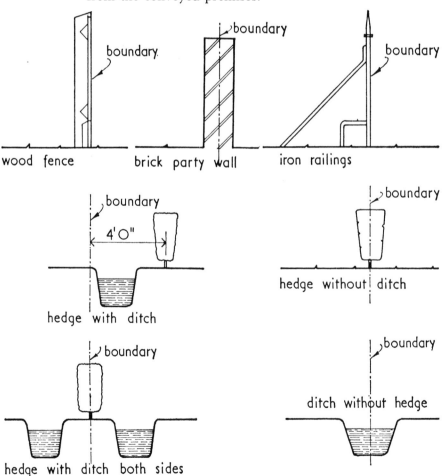

Guide to positioning of boundaries by artifical means (subject to local customs and evidence).

Fences

These are usually fabricated from chestnut or oak, the latter being more durable. Their effective life span is from 20 - 25 years. The posts may be:

○ Driven directly into the ground where they tend to rot fairly quickly.

○ Set into the ground and cased in concrete.

○ Fixed to steel or precast concrete posts driven into the ground or set in concrete.

In good class work gravel boards are provided to the base of the boarding to protect these from contact with the ground and the top is protected by a weathered capping.

Defects include:

○ Rot in the ends of posts causing loss of alignment and eventual collapse of the fence.

○ Rot in the ends of the boards.

Softwood painted 'ranch' fencing and larch lap fencing require regular re-decoration to keep rot at bay. Chestnut spile and wire fencing is primarily a temporary expedient.

Garden walls

Generally of brick but in certain specific areas may be constructed of local materials such as dry stone, chalk clunch, flint and cobbles or cob. In most cases the foundations are very sketchy and where settlement has occurred and the walls have moved out of plumb, piers are constructed which are often not bonded to the wall structure.

Defects in walls may be summarised as:

○ Foundation failure or settlement causing the walls to move out of plumb.

○ Deterioration of the mortar by ground water rising through the wall due to the absence of any damp-resisting membrane.

○ Deterioration of the wall due to failure of the capping to resist water penetration.

○ Pressure exerted on the foundations or wall structure by the proximity of trees or large shrubs.

Deterioration of bedding mortar is common because in most cases this will be a very weak lime mortar unable to withstand a long period of exposure to an increasingly aggressive natural environment. Check the alignment of the wall to ensure that the structure is upright and structurally sound.

Gates

Gates are usually constructed of wood or ferrous material — both being affected by exposure to the elements and generally poorly maintained. Always open and close all gates to see they are openable. Where gates are carried on iron rides built into brick piers, check for rusting of the metal and/or cracking of the brickwork which will cause the pier to fail.

Grounds and gardens

The report should include a short description of:
○ Grounds and gardens, their general standard of planting and general maintenance.
○ Paths and pavings, their construction, and general condition.
○ Vehicular access and driveway, its construction, finish and general condition.
○ The situation of any specimen trees and details of any which, being planted close to the property, might in time cause problems with the foundations.

Garages and outbuildings

Free-standing garages should be inspected and reported in detail in the same manner as the main property. Garage doors are a constant source of trouble and automatic operating gear can be a heavy maintenance charge. Where a service pit is provided check the state and safety of the cover and whether the pit is clean and clear of water.

Greenhouses are a valuable asset, but those constructed of timber are prone to rapid deterioration and collapse through rot. This is usually clearly evident on inspection. Garden sheds, unless patently new, are also generally prone to similar problems.

Finally, the surveyor may well be asked to indicate the height of the property above sea level and its liability to flooding. The height above sea level can usually be found approximately by reference to an Ordnance Survey Map of the area either from spot heights or contours. Liability to flooding is a different matter. Where the property is low-lying and in the immediate vicinity of a river known to flood the answer is simple. Otherwise, inquiry locally or to the local or water authority may be necessary.

Appendix

Building Surveys on New Domestic Properties

Experience indicates that new properties are as liable to defective components as are older buildings. In fact it might be argued that one advantage of purchasing a building no longer in its first youth is that the latent faults have developed and been corrected. While this argument may well be satisfactory for buildings over thirty years old, houses in the ten to fifteen year brackets have services which may well be beginning to show their age and with these problems can develop.

New properties are constructed in accordance with the relevant building legislation in force at the time, and during the construction period the site is visited on occasions by building control officers employed by the local authority for the express purpose of enforcing the regulations respecting the particular building under construction. These regulations generally deal with the following matters:

○ Foundations and general structural stability.
○ Weatherproofing and damp exclusion.
○ Construction of flues, hearths, etc.
○ Fire protection and means of escape (where relevant).
○ Insulation.
○ Provision of adequate and satisfactory water supplies.
○ Drainage and disposal of effluent.

While in most buildings these matters may be generally satisfactory, there are many points of detail and quality, both as regards materials used and workmanship employed which require investigation. The regulations are mainly concerned with standards which may be adequate if great care and skill are exercised, but which fall far short when buildings are constructed without proper and detailed supervision. Many defects occur even when materials, workmanship and method are fully in accordance with statutory requirements. They are to be found in all types of domestic work and, in addition to those matters generally discussed in the main part of this book, the following should be checked with especial care when preparing a structural survey of new domestic properties.

New houses

The roof. Most new houses, especially those in the speculative range, have roof structures composed of trussed rafters whose individual members are secured by patent nailed connectors instead of traditional worked joints. When properly erected these are adequate despite their light scantlings. In many cases, however, such roof structures sag, due to excessive loading or other causes. This is apparent on the ridge which will tend to dip in the middle or between supports. Internally, ceilings will sag and severe cracking may result. One cause of this may be the use of tiles whose deadweight exceeds the design loading. Another may be the omission of roof supports for the cold water cistern, this being carried on the roof members without reinforcement. A third cause may be inadequate design provision for properly trimming trusses around flues passing through the roof, especially if these are near to mid span.

Where roof trusses are provided at specific centres to support purlins and common rafters, the principal problem is movement due to shrinkage in the timbers, producing slackness in the bolted connectors used to join the truss members. This will cause tearing of the timber fibres across the jointed surfaces as the applied load forces the connector out of the timber. Deformation of the truss, settlement of the purlins and sagging of the roof surface will ensue. Trusses should be checked in the roof space for any sign of settlement or twisting, indicating progressive or imminent joint failure.

The walls. Walls faced with exposed brick are generally reasonably safe from initial or progressive defects subject to the employment of proper standards of materials or workmanship. Mortar should be open textured and of a reasonable degree of hardness, neither ironed into the joint nor sandy and soft. The first will produce eventual frost damage to the pointing. In the latter case the use of a mix too lean and short of cement will lead to rapid erosion or to sulphate attack due to the presence of gypsum plaster occasioned by the use of a dirty banker prior to the mixing of mortar for walling.

Damp courses should be checked, especially where paths or landscaping have been carried out as a sales incentive. Those responsible for these works may either ignore or be unaware of the importance of keeping the dpc unbridged and clear of all obstructions.

Walls faced with rendered finishes should be examined for hair cracks which indicate either (1) too rich a mix, or (2) too rapid hardening due to drying out without proper attention being paid to curing, or (3) sulphate attack due to the presence of contaminating gypsum. Renderings should be properly weathered and belled out and undercut at the foot to throw water clear of the wall and prevent staining. Damp courses should not be bridged by any rendered finish and should be exposed on the face of the wall.

Painted finishes on walls should be checked for adhesion and any breakdown due to chemical attack from substances in the substrate or to application over surfaces which had not been allowed to dry out thoroughly.

Weatherboarding should have ends and bottom edges checked for rot. Timber used for this purpose should always be fixed clear of the wall face on battens and include a layer of building paper to allow for a free flow of air to remove condensation which can occur on the backs of the boards in some weather conditions. The backs of all boards should be primed before fixing to seal moisture out.

External joinery is a fruitful source of defects. Omission of priming and paint to the bottom of doors, casements and sill is frequent. Most stock window frames have softwood sills and even where these are treated against rot, horizontal damp courses of felt should be provided to the underside. Putty is usually skimped and open joints both against the glass and in corners will lead to damp penetration to the rebate under the putty, eventually either dislodging it or inducing rot in untreated timber in the sash rebate.

Supports to openings are generally satisfactory but damp proofing over is often inadequate. Weepholes to trays and pressed steel lintel supports are often omitted or blocked and where lead trays are provided these are very rarely properly dressed down over the frame. Felt is never satisfactory and is a likely source of future trouble.

The floors. The stability of timber floors should be adequate because timber sizes will be in accordance with the regulations. Any vibration or undue movement to upper floors is probably due to either shrinkage allowing the blocking between the end joists and the wall at the end of herringbone strutting to fall out, or excessive notching of joists for services. Check the nailing of boarding, two nails to each joist crossing being necessary to provide a proper fixing. If the ground floor is of board and joist construction find and lift an access to see that the space under has been properly cleared out and no timber offcuts are lying on the oversite concrete to provide a possible source for dry rot infestation.

Solid floors should have solidly adhering screeds. If these sound hollow when tapped the screed has lifted from the oversite concrete. Plastic tiles and other in situ finishes should be securely attached to the screed and left clean and in proper condition.

The internal finishes. The presence of plaster cracking is likely because it is probable that the structure is still drying out. These should be mainly located at the junction of ceilings and walls and limited to light cracking in the plaster at the ends of lintels over openings. If this is exceeded, further investigation as described in the chapter on Internal Finishes and Walls is necessary.

The surface of the plaster should be smooth and level, free from rough patches, blow holes and spalling. The density of the paint film gives a good indication of the number of coats applied. If the surface grins through or feels rough to the touch, inadequate coverage is the cause. The presence of hard excrescences or runs on the painted surface indicates inadequate workmanship in applying the paint.

Drainage. The drains will have been tested by the local

authority during the progress of the works. After this has been done, many events can cause defects to occur and consequently the drains of new houses should always be tested during the survey. If this is not possible due to reluctance on the part of the prospective owner to pay the fee and attendance bill, the manhole covers should be opened up and a visual inspection made to check as far as possible the conditions of the drains. The channels of the manholes should be clean and free from silt and when the appliances are flushed water should flow with reasonable rapidity and fully clear through the manhole. Any sluggishness may indicate a backfall in the drain due to settlement or a partly blocked or crushed pipe caused by the passage of heavy vehicles over badly consolidated fill to the drain trenches.

Services. The services should be checked and inspected as previously described. If the property has been empty for any period of time during the winter and there is likelihood of incomplete draining of water through the pipes, a check should be carried out to ascertain whether frost damage has caused splitting of pipes or pulled fittings. The lagging to pipes in the roof spaces should be properly checked, together with storage cistern and hot water cylinder. The interior of the storage cistern should be clean and free from debris and dirt and, if constructed of galvanized iron, the interior should be protected by an application of a black rust inhibitor.

Electrical services are usually satisfactory, the only likely problems being low readings on the megohmeter due to damp or condensation from the drying structure affecting the cables. This is to be expected and is not serious. Check that the earthing is properly effected either by bonding to the main cable or the provision of an earth leakage circuit breaker. Bonding to the cold water main is not satisfactory.

Flats

Flat accomodation is either purpose-built in new blocks or converted from older properties which are too large for single occupation. In either case, of course, it is difficult to examine properly a single flat in a building in multiple occupation or to check out the building as a whole in any detail. It is, however, necessary to give attention to the general construction and applied finishes because in most cases the purchaser of a flat will, through the general imposition of an annual charge, be liable for his share of the maintenance and redecoration of the structure, installed equipment, common ways and exterior finishes. Consequently, a general inspection of the building should be carried out and a short report prepared giving details of the general construction, assessment of the present condition of the finishes and possible maintenance expenditure likely to be incurred in the near future. This is as important with properties that provide for fixed maintenance charges as those whose charges fluctuate from the annual minimum to a proportion of the total cost involved. In the first instance, resistance by the leaseholders to paying any more than the irreducible minimum may result in deterioration of the structure and finishes with a consequential loss of value in the individual properties, and in the second, the incorporation in the building of materials of high maintenance potential may render the purchaser liable to higher charges than originally estimated.

New flats. Defects and problems that may be found in new houses generally occur in new blocks of flats although infestation by beetle or defects induced by dry rot are less likely because of the general use of concrete for ground and intermediate compartmenting floors to meet the requirements of the Building Regulations. A similar concrete construction for flat roofs is also common for this type of development. Procedures for carrying out the inspection and preparing the report should follow those generally recommended in the individual chapters of this book. So far as the structure is concerned, the report will, of necessity, be briefer and less detailed than that for an entire property. Internally, attention must be directed to the finishes, joinery and fittings forming part of the flat and at the same time special care must be taken to consider and comment on matters that will affect the safety and comfort of the prospective owner. These may be summarised as:

1. *Fire protection*
(a) Check that the rwp's, one-pipe stacks and all vertical service duct runs are properly protected to ensure that fire will not pass from one flat to another by these routes.
(b) Check that the external door from the flat to the common

ways is of solid construction indicating compliance with half-hour fire resistance requirements, that the rebates are at least 1in (25mm) deep and if planted on are screwed and not nailed. These doors should be provided with a proper self-closing device (rising butts are not suitable or efficient for this purpose) and be fitted with an antislam lock to prevent the owner being locked out of the flat in an emergency. Any delivery or meter cupboards provided as a part of the door assembly should have the same degree of fire resistance and be fitted with the same or similar self-closing devices as the main entrance door.

2. Sound insulation
Despite the regulations, this is often inefficient both for impact or air transmitted noise. Simple and obvious on-the-spot checks can be applied. Mechanical or other noises may also be noticed during the inspection if at all unduly obtrusive. The position of the lift shaft in relation to the compartmenting walls of the flat should be checked. The noise of lift motors and the closing of lift doors can be considerable and even intolerable if close or adjacent to bedrooms.

Services and installations in some blocks are complex, in others almost non-existent. The provision of a central boiler plant may well be considered a convenience by some, but unless the service to individual flats is metered, and preferably individually controlled, problems may arise. Degrees of temperature comfort vary widely between individuals. Main service ducts under floors, unless adequately insulated, can raise temperatures to intolerable levels in the flats concerned. The provision of heat meters ensures that the apportionment of cost is fairly distributed between the owners. In any event, circuits within the flat should be within the personal control of the individual owner and controlling thermostat should be provided to meet individual levels of heating and comfort.

Similar control provision should be made for hot and cold water services. Each flat should be provided with valves to isolate circuits within its compartmenting walls so that the owner can shut off his own services in an emergency without causing a complete shutdown for the whole building. Care should be taken to investigate and report on service control provision within the flat and any deficiencies should be included in the report.

Lifts are a great boon to the elderly, especially in buildings of any height. They do, however, require regular maintenance and the renewal of machinery, especially ropes, at intervals during the life of the building. The cost of these renewals is considerable and can be a serious burden on the maintenance charges. Details of the lift maintenance agreement and dates of reroping should be requested from the agents so that any high or abnormal expenditure can be assessed by the prospective purchaser before completion of the contract.

The provision of refuse chutes is common practice in many areas and blocks of flats are often provided with these useful devices. The covenants of the lease should include a clause requiring all matter to be sealed in a stout bag before being placed in the chute. Otherwise the pipe will become fouled and odorous. Contamination of this nature is extremely difficult to remedy. Inspection of the chute by removing the cover will indicate whether the installation is satisfactory and proper sanitary precautions are being taken.

Flats converted from older buildings. Much of what has been written applies also to converted premises. Often the potential problems are greater due to the complexities of the structure and the existence of older and consequently more vulnerable finishes.

Fire protection and sound insulation are serious matters and should be investigated with care. Timber floors are usually adequately protected on the underside by a plastered ceiling. If originally straight-edged floor boarding has been used, it should heve been covered during the conversion by a layer of 1/8in (3.2mm) hardboard to seal the gaps between the boards. This hardboard is not always adequately fixed with pins or brads at 6in (150mm) centres and the board should be checked for proper fixing.

Lightweight timber floor construction rarely incorporates pugging between the joists to reduce sound transmission, reliance being wholly placed on applied finishings provided by the occupier. The covenants included in the lease should be checked to see what is required in this respect, and during the inspection attention should be paid to gauge the effectiveness of sound deadening by surface finishings provided by other occupiers.

Care must be taken to inspect the services. Usually these are completely renewed during the conversion, but sometimes they are merely adapted and trouble can occur with the retention of old lead and galvanised iron pipes. Control is important as in new flats. With high ceilings and large rooms, heating is often inadequate, provided on a minimum basis only. Check that the heating is adequate for normal conditions without the risk of overloading.

Specimen
Report prepared on the structural condition of Flat No. 10, Bramber House, Michel Grove, Eastbourne, East Sussex, following an inspection carried out on Monday, 20 December 1976.

PRIVATE AND CONFIDENTIAL
1.00 *General description.* The property comprises a self-contained flat situated on the fifth floor of a block of flats originally constructed in about 1962. The flat on the top fifth floor has accommodation comprising lounge, study opening off a small balcony, two bedrooms, bathroom and separate wc/cloakroom, kitchen and entrance hall. In addition there is a single garage forming part of a block together with an external store. The property is situated on the NW side of Michel Grove backing on to Upperton Road.

2.00 *The roof.* The roof to the property is of pitched construction with a flat forming the centre of the roof area. The construction is of a timber, the sloping roof surfaces being finished with handmade clay plain tiles on battens and sarking felt, the flat areas being boarded over and, if similar properties in the road are anything to go by, the finish is asphalt. There are several tiles missing from the general roof slopes.
2.01 The eaves to the property project from 6in to 2ft proud of the wall face and are provided with boarded soffits and fascia. There does not appear to be any movement in the roof structure showing in the eaves.
2.02 The gutters to the block are cast iron ogee pattern and are rusty inside and will need much cleaning down on the

next painting. They appear to be adequate to serve the roof areas.

2.03 The rain water pipes are 3in cast iron. That which discharges into the gully on the balcony of the flat does in fact spill over and flood the balcony. The rain water pipe should discharge below the gully grating to be effective.

2.04 Access into the roof space is from the ceiling hatch immediately outside the entrance door to Flat 9. The other access is into the lift motor room. From the hatch the roof could be seen to be well constructed of clean sound timber. Inspection of the roof was perfunctory but the area was clean and no sign of infestation could be seen in adjoining timbers at the time of the inspection. As far as could be seen there was no water penetration through the roof covering at the time of the inspection.

2.05 The ceilings of the flats on the top floor are of plasterboard finished with plaster skim and with fibreglass insulation between the timber ceiling joists.

3.00 *The walls.* The external walls are generally of cavity construction, mostly faced with Sussex stock bricks but with small areas of Tyrolean rendering to the balconies and some red clay tile hanging to the gables. The external finishing is in good condition and the brickwork pointing is satisfactory.

3.01 The flats are provided each with a small balcony constructed of concrete and weathered with asphalt. The balcony to Flat 10 is provided with a small area of asbestos tiles which are no longer solidly bedded, water having penetrated underneath. The iron balustrade is loose at the NW end and the plastic facing is damaged.

3.02 The windows to the block are mostly standard stock joinery finished with gloss paint. Opening lights are either side or top hung. The opening lights are badly fitting and have either been weatherstripped with metal strips or a separate double glazing unit has been supplied and fixed to the inside of the frames. The sills to the windows are hardwood left natural. The condition of the windows is reasonable but the bottoms of the glazed lights have been affected by condensation and small areas of wet rot occur as follows:

(*a*)   To the side hung casement to the main lounge window.
(*b*)   To the window of the principal bedroom.
(*c*)   To the small window of the bathroom on the left-hand

side.

(*d*)   To the kitchen window.

3.03 The external doors to the flat are of timber, the interior door is of fireproof construction in accordance with the regulations, the exterior door is of timber, glazed in two lights. Both the bottom and the lock rail are affected by wet rot.

3.04 The glass and putties of the windows and doors are generally sound.

4.00 *Internal finishes.* The ceilings are plastered as mentioned before and there is some shrinkage cracking around the edges of the sheets which will need filling before redecoration. The walls are papered over plaster finish and need some filling where fittings have been or are to be removed. I would suggest that the ceiling should be lined before emulsion is applied and that the wallpaper be removed and the walls relined before emulsion to obtain a good finish.

4.01 The woodwork is standard stock work generally and with the painted finish is in reasonable condition.

4.02 The stains in the flat are, in my opinion, due to condensation caused by lack of heating and ventilation during the last tenancy. The walls were dry at the time of the inspection. The reveal at the left-hand side of the lounge window is damp under the gloss finish.

5.00 *The floors.* The floors of the whole block are of concrete construction finished with cement screed on which the carpets and sheet flooring are laid. The floors would have been designed to the loadings permitted under the Building Bylaws applicable at the time of construction.

5.01 The stairs serving the block are of reinforced concrete construction finished with thermoplastic tiles over a cement screed. The stability and construction appear to be adequate.

5.02 In my opinion each landing should be separated from the common stair by a fire-resisting door to prevent smoke dispersal throughout the building in the event of a fire. The doors should be fitted with an approved self-closing device.

6.00 *The drainage.* Drainage from the flat is through a soil and vent shaft situated in the corner of the wc. This is likely to be cast iron of 4in diameter and as such would be quite satisfactory. The traps to the fittings where visible are copper or chrome and the wastes are of copper. The system appeared to be in working order.

6.01 Discharge from the soil stacks will be to the local authority sewers.

7.00 *Installations.* Main water enters the flat under the sink where is provided a stop cock. The main will be common to all flats on the side of the block. The size of the rising main could not be ascertained as it was buried under the fitting.

7.01 The cold water down service to the five flats on the side of the block runs down in the linen cupboard. The connections to the flat are provided with isolating valves. Supplies to each flat are, therefore, not independent.

7.02 Hot water is provided by a copper hot water cylinder in the linen cupboard served in a similar manner from block cold water storage situated in the roof space. An isolating valve is provided to isolate the flat from the supply. The cylinder is provided with an electric immersion heater and the cylinder is lagged.

7.03 A gas supply is laid on into the service cupboard by the flat front door. The supply is capped off at this point.

7.04 The electrical installation is wired in PVC cable and appears to be perfectly satisfactory.

7.05 Heating is by electric storage heaters which are neither placed properly to warm the flat nor adequate to supply sufficient heat as required for modern standards of comfort.

7.06 Refuse disposal is provided by a refuse chute situated in the entrance hall by the lift doors. The flue runs through the roof space and discharges to vent to open air through the roof in the usual manner.

7.07 Although the lift appears to be well maintained and quiet, the noise of its operation and motor noise could be heard from within the flat with the front door closed.

20 December 1976

Jack Bowyer
FRIBA Architect

Index